My Father's Book

THE SWISS LIST

My Father's Book

URS WIDMER

TRANSLATED BY DONAL MCLAUGHLIN

LONDON NEW YORK CALCUTTA

swiss arts council

prɔhelvetia

This publication was supported by a grant from Pro
Helvetia, Swiss Arts Council

Seagull Books, 2017

First publshed as *Das Buch des Vaters* by Urs Widmer
© Diogenes Verlag AG, Zurich, Switzerland 2005

English translation © Donal McLaughlin 2011

First published in English translation by Seagull Books, 2011

ISBN 978 0 8574 2 527 0

Typeset by Seagull Books, Calcutta, India
Printed by Hyam Enterprises, Calcutta, India

For May

MY FATHER WAS A COMMUNIST. He'd not always been a communist, of course not, and no longer was when he died. To be precise, he was a member of the Communist Party for only a few years, from 1944 until about 1950. Thereafter, his disgust crossed all party lines, and he'd rail against all politicians, pretty much all of them. 'Stupid ass! Halfwit! Murderer!'—That he would become a communist no one could have foreseen. *His* father read just one book all his life, the Bible—his mother knew the Bible, too, but only from hearsay—and didn't bother about political matters, a vague enthusiasm for Kaiser Wilhelm II apart. As a ten-year-old, my father really had gone to the barracks with his Papa, or rather, to the drill ground behind them, because the Kaiser of All the Germans was visiting his neighbouring country, and its most beautiful town, and was taking the salute of its troops. A magnificent blue sky, Kaiser weather, simply. A good-humoured crowd. My father, small for his age, was allowed to join the children at the front and, over the heads of other boys and girls, saw a group of horsemen trot past in splendid uniforms, very close, each with a different head-dress. Gold helmets, red plumes, spiked helmets, caps decorated with oak leaves aplenty. The boys and girls around him shouted with glee and threw their caps in the air. My father, too, was burning with enthusiasm. The only thing was: he didn't know which of the ones with plumes was the Kaiser. Him on the white horse, or maybe it *was* him with the twirly moustache? He didn't dare ask his neighbour, a fat lad, blocking his view. — On the way home, he got a sugared doughnut and he and his father raved about how magnificent the monarch had looked. — A year later, when the First World War broke out, my father's father — a quiet man — was still shouting *Hooray* and *Let them have it*; everyone in the town was, pretty much. Anything to do with French-speaking Switzerland wasn't highly regarded back then, and my father read *Der gute Kamerad*, a magazine that always had front-page pictures of warships, firing from all their barrels, or of soldiers charging from the trenches, roaring. — Apart from that, he noticed very little about the war, my father; at most, that his father's enthusiasm for it was becoming less and less and, in the end, completely vanished. — His mother said not a word about what was happening in the war. — My father went to the grammar school behind the cathedral, learnt ancient Greek and Latin, was always top of the class, without trying. At home, though, he was always the stupid one, as his brother, Felix, was always two years ahead of him and, in his class, was the even-more-undisputed top pupil. If my father had 6s across the board, and a 5.5 only in PT, then Felix would have the top grade in that subject, too, in his report. (To say nothing of the marks for application and conduct, my father's Achilles heel.) At the same time, my

father was a better footballer than Felix, which is to say, Felix
wasn't a footballer at all. He kept his nose in his books that, in
his case, remained immaculate, even if he read them ten times.
My father became a prolific goalscorer with the Old Boys' jun-
ior team, he played at centre-forward and was known as the little one with the unstoppable shot. — Maybe he only called
himself that. — Politics, he was oblivious to. The roar of the
cannons at Ypres and Verdun was far off. He didn't even run
into Lenin, though this could well have happened, for the
future revolutionary walked the same streets. Maybe — as he
later occasionally thought — he *had* seen him: him, with a football under his arm; Lenin, all in black, ranting to himself. His
heart hadn't raced to tell him he'd just spotted his idol, his later
idol. — That the General Strike was happening, he did, definitely, realize. He was now sixteen and could hear, in the
distance, on Münsterplatz, the shooting and screaming. His
street empty, so empty he wouldn't leave the house. He heard
about the Revolution in Russia too, *en passant*. Much more
threatening was the influenza, raging at the time through the
town. His grandfather — his mother's father — died of it; as did
Uncle Max. A distant great-cousin, too, he'd hardly known.
His parents, tear-stained. — In the Twenties, the most political
thing he did was to join a fraternity regarded as progressive
because the students didn't take swords to one another's heads
till they drew blood. On the contrary: the duelling fraternities,
the ones with the cuts on their faces, were the enemy. And
when, of an evening, his fraternity was at its usual table in
Restaurant Harmonie, clunking their tankards at each toast,
they'd get worked up about the fact that the high offices of state,
and places on the supervisory boards of the largest companies,
always fell to the so-called Elder Gentlemen from the Helvetia
or Rhenania fraternities, the now-graduated, fat little sons of

bourgeois families, with scabs on their cheeks. The members
of Zofingia, to which my father belonged, were the sons of car-
penters, fitters, railwaymen. (My father's father was a primary-
school teacher.) They were convinced that *they*, one day, one
day soon, would be sitting at the levers of power and
then *they*'d be kicking those rich, mollycoddled kids on the
behind. — There were still no women, in those days. — Only in
the Thirties did my father have his first contact with communists. He was now about thirty, and had become a young
intellectual. He looked it, too: glasses, a receding hairline, cigarette at the corner of his mouth. He was always smoking,
even when he was speaking, reading or eating, and his new
friends, the communists, asked him how he managed to sleep
or kiss, ever. No problem, my father answered. He didn't kiss
a lot, he told them, and slept even less. His friends smoked,
too, and they drank, unlike my father, with relish and a lot.
They were all painters — only one of them was an architect —
and, a year or two before my father met them — had formed a
group, named after the year in which it was founded. Thirty-
three. My father, who didn't paint, became their secretary, as it
were. He took care of the group's coffers — him, of all people! —
and tried to persuade gallery owners to exhibit his friends'
paintings. In the evenings, they would sit in the Ristorante
Ticino, a restaurant behind the freightyard, a place they all
called the Thieves' Den, 'den' because the lumpen proletariat,
easy girls and artists felt at ease there. The landlord was called
Luigi; was, indeed, from the Ticino — from the Maggia Valley;
and was a hot-blooded comrade. Sometimes, from behind the
counter, he'd sing the songs of his home region, or the *Internationale*, and the whole place would sing along. The painters
and my father would speak about African art and Picasso and
the Surrealists; and about the dictatorship of the proletariat

that would put a stop to the blatant injustices of the bourgeoisie. The rise of Hitler frightened them, and they joked about him a lot. The more shameless Hitler's actions became, the more Stalin became a shining hero to them; they didn't joke about him. They heard about the show trials, of course. But considered what they heard to be smears. (The war then made Stalin completely unassailable. Who, if not him, could stand up to the monster that was Hitler? The victory at Stalingrad even bore his name, and was the first sign the Nazis would lose their war.) Not even now did my father think to join the Communist Party, though nearly all his painter friends had their membership book in their pockets. The war in Spain! Two of the painters had barely heard of Franco's putsch when they'd set off on their bikes and joined the fight in Toledo. One of them had returned and, without a word, taken a seat at their table again. He hadn't changed any; except now he didn't speak a word. Not a single syllable about his friend, about what had happened to him. Three days later he was arrested and taken away, from the table, and sentenced by a military court to five months in prison because, though a Swiss soldier, he'd done war service in a foreign army. My father, who thought Switzerland would thank its heroes for wishing to defend democracy, now travelled every Wednesday to Lenzburg, or perhaps it was Aarburg, to one of the military prisons, in any case, and took the painter cigarettes, chocolate and paints. The latter still said nothing, merely smoked in sombre fashion. Only once did he growl at my father to forget the paints. He'd never paint again. — Now my father was ready for the Party. But only once it was banned, at the beginning of the World War, did he feel as if he were a member, and he did indeed join immediately when it was legalized again, in 1944, a year before the end of the war. The

Party simply couldn't have the same name, that is, Communist Party, and so called itself the Swiss Party of Labour. His friends, naturally, were again — or still — members. One of the painters — who'd learnt a lot from Ernst Ludwig Kirchner but also rated the optimism of the Soviet Realists — and the architect stood for the town council, and my father had allowed himself to be persuaded, too, to take a low place on the list. 'Don't worry, there's no chance of being elected that far down!' He even gave a speech, at the Volkshaus, and was impressed by how easy he found it. To be honest, he'd only shouted 'Comrades!' when thunderous applause broke out. So he'd shouted 'Comrades' again, and, later, another four or five times, when his thoughts about the plight of education in the town began to stutter. — The elections not only ended with the Social Democrats being the strongest party in the town but also made a political force of the communists who, until recently, had still been raising their fists in rear rooms with the curtains closed. Eighteen seats, at the first go. My father, who'd been nineteenth on the list, had come that close to being elected. He was now the first fall-back candidate and had to be ready to take a seat on the council if a councillor died. But none of them did. — The Swiss Party of Labour even succeeded in getting one of their comrades onto the Federal Council. He had the smallest and most unpopular department, and was responsible for the trams and the schools, a combination, the sense, or lack of which, no one could explain any more. When, after the election, my father went to his office, hoping to set about the school reform he'd promised the voters, Comrade Federal Councillor was sitting at his empty desk, pushing a miniature tram back and forth, a true-to-life model he'd received as a present from the Public Services Union. He looked at my father, blankly. School reform, yes, of course, the school reform. Clearly, clearly. But he'd now been elected, that was what was most important, surely. He smiled at his tram. My father left the office, slamming the door, because he slammed the doors of all the rooms he got annoyed in. He was still foaming when he turned up at the restaurant, and the pupil of Kirchner and the architect, both now members of the town council, needed quite some time to calm him down. That evening, he drank more than usual, considerably more, and at closing time was so drunk that the architect went to the telephone box, next to the railway underpass, and called my father's wife. She'd have to help him home. She came almost immediately, by bike, got a hold of my father under his arms and dragged him—the bike on one side, my father on the other—home. My father had a gigantic bunch of roses with him that he was clasping with both hands. She asked him who the roses were for, but he simply giggled and exclaimed how gorgeously beautiful she was, how he loved her, and that he was going to tell her, right now, what he'd thought the first time he'd seen her. She knew already, of course. 'What, then?'—'A vision!' My father had seen her, outside the Sommercasino, getting out of a car, in a white evening dress and with a hat as big as an umbrella, almost. Red lips, black hair that flowed down her back. It was as if he'd been struck by lightning, and he'd known right away: it's her, or no one. 'You or no one,' he chuckled, taking such a sudden step to the side that the bike fell over. 'There and then, I knew it.'—When he met her again a few years later, again outside the Sommercasino—albeit she wasn't in a car, and not wearing a hat either—he asked her, even before she'd reached the gate, would she have a glass of lemonade with him, a glass of champagne, and when she looked, all serious, into his eyes and then smiled, would she marry him? She became all serious again, looked again with those big dark eyes, and said yes. He introduced himself — 'Karl! — and asked what her name was. She was called Clara, Clara Molinari. The champagne had arrived meanwhile, and they both emptied their glass without a word. She knew him, Karl, this wasn't them just meeting, Clara then said. She'd seen him — in another life — a few times already, at the concerts, always with beautiful young women, a different one each time, and then once in the Bayerische Bierhalle, where she'd had a glass of wine with her best friend, a cellist. He'd been with all his ladies at once, three of them, and had cracked one joke after another. Huge guffaws. She'd laughed too, and her friend even more; much more. — 'No beer, in a Bavarian Beer Hall?' my father said. 'No man?' — 'No man, no beer.' — They married, maybe not quite that same evening, but it was an emergency, kind of. Only the cellist was with them when they went to the registry office, and Felix, his brother. — My father was overjoyed and carried his wife over the threshold of his bachelor pad. On their wedding night — no, before — they looked at photos, sitting beside one another on my father's daybed. Clara had brought them in a blue cardboard box, for my father to get to know her better. And so he got to see Clara's father, a strict man with a black beard, and her mother, who looked more gentle. 'Two weeks later, she died.' A spotted cat that was dead too; and the house, a villa that didn't exist any more either. Clara, in a summer dress, leaning against her car, her father's car, a Fiat. (The Fiat was gone too.) Her sister, deer-like. Uncles like gnomes and blocks of rock, standing among vines. Aunts in mourning. A cousin who had a mountain rope round his shoulders and an ice pick in his hand. — At the very bottom of the box lay a large-format photo. 'The visit of the Kaiser.' — 'The Kaiser? Which one's the Kaiser?' — 'Him there, of course.' My father saw him — 'Oh, right? Him!'—with plumes on his head, mounted on his horse, surrounded by similarly mounted adjutants and the high officers of the Swiss Army. Behind them, stiff and well-behaved, a crowd. Clara pointed to a serious little girl in the first row, looking into the camera. 'I'm her!'—My father bent over the picture. He looked, even taking his glasses off. He then pointed, with a red face, to the half of the head of a boy looking out from behind the shoulders of a cloddish lad with a flat cap, and said, 'And I'm him!'

THE EVENING BEFORE THE MORNING MY FATHER DIED I was at the circus with a couple we were friendly with, Max and Eva, and my mother. When we were leaving—my mother was sweeping up and down the stairs—my father came out of his room, yellow, and even more transparent than usual, looked at me with big eyes, and moved his lips. 'What?' I said. He repeated what he'd said, and, as I leant towards him and watched his lips, this time I understood him. 'Don't go. I'm not well,' he said. He was wearing his cardigan—it was summer!—was holding his cigarette in one hand, and, behind the lenses of his glasses, his eyes were wet. I hugged him—he'd not been well for years—and said, 'But Papa, we've tickets for the circus, as you know—and Eva and Max are waiting for us.' He nodded. 'We'll be back by eleven, at the latest.'—It was a good show—a great trapeze act, caramel-coloured horses that waltzed on their hind legs and clowns that were downright funny—and at ten to eleven we were back home. My father was already asleep, at least I didn't hear anything when I listened at his door, neither his breathing nor the coughing that kept waking him and, often, us too. My room was directly above his. It had always been my room for I'd never moved out, though twenty-seven meanwhile, because I thought it would kill my father. He was so wretched, so sore. He reminded me of a mouse, caught in a cage of books; of a skinned mouse. The slightest touch hurt him, every kiss, every hug; and so he barely moved, himself, any more. Across to the bathroom to swallow a painkiller, to the loo, that was as far as he went. I couldn't think of what to do, other than to go to him at times and watch, in silence, as he wrote. It didn't disturb him. He'd a typewriter, on which, with one finger, the index finger of his right hand, he typed at a furious speed. Before he went to bed, he wrote—every evening, even when travelling, or after a party that had gone on until the early morning—with a quill pen and ink in a book that was bound in black leather, in a tome full of once-empty pages, just about all of which he'd covered with writing meanwhile. He'd been doing this for half a century. It was an assignment; he, at any rate, couldn't do any different. He'd such small handwriting that a page was enough for several days. He wrote without a reading glass, bowed way down over the page, but perhaps not even *he* could read what was written there. The old pages, from forty or fifty years ago, he too had to divine. His writing was precise; every line dead straight. The largest letter was a millimetre. I'd once asked him, a single once, what he was writing. 'The book of my life,' he'd answered. —Whenever I came into the room, he'd say 'Take a sweet,' and he kept saying it long after I was past the age when there's nothing you love more than sweet stuff. And so I would open the bottom drawer of the desk and take a raspberry or lemon sweet from a large jar. My father would look at me, without stopping writing. —In the other drawers, if—for once—I opened them, or rather, if I peeked in when my father did, were quills, ink jars, papers, clips. Envelopes, stamps, rubbers. The top drawer, however, was locked. His secret things were in there. — I'd difficulty falling asleep that evening, then bad dreams tormented me. While in a deep sleep I heard a sound from the room below, as if a bough were breaking, and — still asleep — bolted out of bed and flew downstairs before I was properly awake. I pushed open the door to my father's room. He was lying in the wet area, his head bent beneath the basin, at a slant against the bath. He was breathing, rattling, with faltering gasps. I knew: this was death. His cigarette was hanging between the fingers of his right hand. I threw it in the bath. Kneeling over him, I got him by the arms and dragged him out from under the basin. Let him go again, because water shot out of the tap and I'd to turn it off again; and pulled at him as he'd managed to jam himself between the basin, the bath and the wall. When I freed his head, his legs got tangled up in the rods of the clothes horse. Somehow, I managed to drag him across to his room, like a sack, and heave him onto his bed. He was so small, and yet so heavy! His glasses were lying on the carpet, in two bits. Maybe I'd stood on them. 'Papa,' I said. He was no longer breathing and had his mouth open. He was dead. On one temple there was blood, where he'd crashed against the wall. I fetched a towel and put it on the wound. Outside, beyond the window, morning was breaking. I went to the telephone and called Dr Grien, his family doctor and friend of many decades, with whom, however — only recently — he'd fallen out, I don't know why. Probably Dr Grien had again suggested that the many cigarettes — yes, four packets a day — was a very high dose, blue Gauloises into the bargain, and what if he were to have only one pack, or none at all? and my father had slammed all the doors, of course, but, for sure, not without first telling him, more clearly than ever, what he could lick, and from top to bottom at that, and till the end of time. He told him where to shove his medical qualification too. 'I'm not his doctor any more,' Dr Grien said, with the voice of a man who had just gone into a deep sleep and had now been irretrievably wakened. 'As you know. As he knows, at any rate.' — 'It's for the last time,' I said. Ten minutes later Dr Grien was there, he in his pyjamas, too, over which he was wearing a raincoat, and with slippers on his bare feet. He shone a little lamp in my father's eyes, felt his pulse and sighed. 'Oh well,' he said. 'I'm sorry.' He lifted his case, an old leather bag, and left. My mother was there now, too. She was standing at the foot of the bed, as white as chalk, in a grey nightdress. I'd sat down on the chair at my father's desk — I'd never done that — and was looking at the page in his book on which he'd just been writing. He'd not managed to finish the last sentence, there was no full stop, in any case. I leafed through the book. Every page was so full, the lines of writing so tight that there wasn't a spot of white. Ten, fifteen pages had remained empty. White. He'd died before his time. — The book resembled a bible, it was so massive, so black. No cross embossed on the leather of the cover, it's true, but gilt edging at the top and a frayed pale ribbon for marking the place. I put it between the final pages and went out past my mother. As I closed the door, she was bending over her husband and, with two fingers, closing his eyes. In her other hand, she was holding one side of his glasses; the lens had a jagged crack through it, like lightning.

MY FATHER WAS A BIG BOY when — not for the first time, but for the first time alone — he took the path from his house in the town to the village his father and mother came from. His actual goal was the village church, known as the Black

Chapel, though it was white, rather; externally, at least; and also had quite a tower, a nave, and just the hint of a transept, a small one. His ancestors' village and the church were situated in the mid-mountains, a day's walk away. The house in town was in the so-called bog, a part of town, not boggy at all, at the end of the lake basin, and full of small, narrow, terraced houses. Space was tight in my father's childhood home, too. But it had windows that shone, with green shutters, and was squeezed between two cheerful houses. My father set off early in the morning, the sun on his back. He knew he'd to go the same way as it, at the same speed. It was his birthday, his twelfth, and he was wearing the ritual garments that had been laid out, ready for his walk, for some time. Solid shoes with nailed soles, black trousers, a jacket, a white shirt. The kind of hat an apprentice would wear, which made him older than he was. A leather sack, with some bread, cheese and a bottle of cider in it—they, too, time-honoured provisions for the way. The sack was the one his father had carried on *his* way to the Chapel; his route, though, having just been across the square; presumably, his father's father had hung it over his shoulder, too. The sky was a radiant blue, the sun tempting every possible colour out of the washed-out walls of the houses. Yellow, sienna red, olive green. Shadows were dancing beneath trees. The air, gentle. Karl waved to his parents who were both at the front door, their arms raised, then hopped along behind a horse-drawn cart, loaded with chunks of ice that had a blue glow. Snow-melt sprayed onto his shoes, not that the blocks of ice were becoming any smaller. A greengrocer was setting out tomatoes and lettuces on a long table. He called out to Karl, who laughed and hopped onwards. He passed the brewery, the local factory, its halls all made of the same brick, its main building resembling a castle. Soon, he was at the moat and redoubts, where two lovers were walking hand in hand and gardeners were watering their roses. Behind the Old Customs—the name of an inn; beneath blossoming chestnuts, two men were having their first beer of the day—began the forest, and, already, my father was trotting along between beeches and oaks that were shining so much that their green was dancing on the black of his jacket. There was bird call; an early cuckoo, too. Karl mimicked it, the others also, and got a response each time. He shouted with glee. He cut himself a hazel stick and hit out against any broom and elder bushes. A fat bird flew up out of one, fluttered—heavily—off. The path was now climbing, gently, its broad bends leading up the hill. Soon there were firs, too, which were darker and which, where there were groups of them, prevented the sun from reaching the ground. Beneath them, a carpet of brown needles. The scent of resin. Karl kicked a pine cone ahead until it disappeared into the nettles. Far ahead leapt a deer. Karl was sweating now, the path had become steep and the sun was directly above him. The beech trees were left behind now; the oaks too; only firs now, almost, mightier ones that concealed the sky more and more. The path became a track where tall stalks grew, blackberry twines that hooked themselves to his jacket and trousers. A thorn badly scratched Karl's hand, but he didn't bother about the spot of blood; instead, he whistled a song for he was sure he was on the track he'd taken with his father the year before. 'There, remember that crooked tree, the rock with the moss on it, next year you'll have to walk alone.' At the foot of the rock was something like a small quarry, full of glittering pebbles; Karl pocketed a few handfuls. He reached the first patches of snow, from which pale alpine snowbells were growing and snow-melt flowed. His shoes crunched in the crusted snow, made dirty footprints.

Stones covered in lichen. Crocuses. Butterflies fluttering; moths, more like. The sun had overtaken my father and was shining in his face. It had grown colder. My father sat down on a tree stump—dark treetops all around—and took the bread, the cheese and the cider from the leather sack. He ate. Birds, mountain finches maybe, pecked up the crumbs. Karl threw them the bits of cheese that were left over and jumped to his feet. The sun now had a start, was hanging in the sky diagonally ahead of him. He followed it, as fast as he could. More and more ancient stone pines, motionless birds on the branches. Griffins, perhaps; vultures. Gloomier light. The path was still visible, at least, even if only people like Karl were walking it, for those who had headed home earlier— they, too, from the town; they, too, on their twelfth birthdays—had dropped, here and there, those little shining stones which Karl, too, was now throwing ahead. They reflected the least piece of sunlight and pointed the way. That said, clouds were now pushing their way in, in front of the sun. A wind came up and shook the branches. In no time Karl was feeling the first drops of a rain that was soon teeming down, as if it wanted to drown him. It had become dark, there were flashes of lightning, to the left, to the right; for seconds, they lit up the stones pointing the way. Thunder roared; hailstones soon, too, dancing around Karl. Fortunately, he could still hear his father's advice who had impressed upon him, 'Hail, should it hail—and it always does—then take your jacket off and put it, like a cushion, under your hat. You'll freeze. You'll freeze as never before. But the ice that comes crashing from the sky won't be able to harm you.' And so my father wrapped the jacket like a turban round his skull, put his hat on top of it, and, true enough, right away, he was freezing. His teeth were chattering. In no time his shirt was soaking wet, sticking to his skin. It froze, stiffened. Hailstones were hitting his head and bouncing off the ground. Hugging himself, he jumped each time to avoid the lightning. He was running now. Was it the right path? He implored the spirits to make him go the right way, without the sun now, without its light that made the stones gleam; the flashes of lightning were confusing him, and not helping, he could equally easily head towards that ravine or this cleft in the rock. Once, with one foot in a small marsh and the other tangled in vines, he called for help, 'Help!'—a quiet little voice amid a din that would have drowned out more powerful cries. And yet, barely a minute later, the rain eased off and petered out. Lightning flashed two or three times in the distance, and the thunder rolled off until only a distant rumbling remained. The sky opened up again. A pale light. Karl was now walking along the stream that came from the village, on a track that, on the side where the stream was, had a railing. Crashing and foaming, the water was, but he now knew where he was again. When he stepped round a white chalk rock—it grew out of the near-black pasture land, and looked like a giant's hand, with four fingers reaching into the sky—he saw the village. The barns supported by what looked like porcini, and the houses, all built with ancient wood and with tiny, slit-like windows. The sun was now low, behind their silhouettes. Karl breathed in, and out again. He'd done it! He'd not been slower than the sun, after all; not a lot, anyway. He waved to it, and it sank so quickly behind the roofs that you'd have thought someone was pulling it down into the abyss. Its final ray, from deep down, lit, for a brief moment, the church weathercock as it looked over the gable of a house that was closer. Karl walked in that direction—where the cock was the church had to be—along a lane on which round stones had been carefully laid, but which, nonetheless, went this way, then that, and up and down. Like a fossilized wave. Between the houses nettles were growing, and puddles in the middle of the path were giving off a smell. Acrid. Piss. Mule piss. Karl stepped from one dry stone to the next, and yet, more than once, ended up in the stinking brew. Finally, his shoes all smeared, he reached the church square. The sun had gone, but the sky was casting the last of its light on houses the height of castles that stood in a semicircle and, like Karl now, too, looked down over the steeply descending cobblestones, towards the restaurant and church that, far below, stood as if on a stage, the church at its right-hand, and the restaurant at its left-hand, edge. The mules were there, too, tied to stakes and wooden poles, their heads in their nose-bags. Karl imme-diately saw the coffins, too. He'd known about them, just as he'd known about the mules, and so didn't get a fright, not at all, almost, when he saw the first of them outside one of the houses. Three people-length boxes, next to one another. He looked from house to house. Outside every — really, every! — one, were coffins like this, most made of old weather-beaten wood, but a few, too, were bright and freshly planed. They were piled carefully — here, five or ten; there, only two — on top of one another, and all lined up. Outside this house or that, though — the one Karl was outside, for instance, its door was askew, and its unglazed windows were boarded up with shin-gles — the coffins had been thrown any which way on top of one another. 'With the coffins, it's the same as with the dunghills in the Emmental,' Karl's father had said. 'You see the pile, and you know what the people who live there are like!' He, for example, would never have married a woman from a house with carelessly piled coffins. — Everyone in the village, when they were born, was given a coffin, in which they were then laid when their time came. Until then, the coffin waited outside the house. Every man had his coffin, every woman hers. There was no such thing as a villager, man or woman, without a coffin. Karl had been given his, too, of course. He could see it in the middle of the pile outside the inn, a veritable mountain range of coffins: a box made of planed, almost red, wood that, by now, was almost as colourless as all the other coffin woods. The inn's landlord who, in one corner of the bar, also ran the village post office, was his uncle. His father's brother. So many people were linked to him, and his house, that the coffins surrounded the house like a wall. At his uncle's place lived countless great aunts, and third cousins of both genders. They alone accounted for a dozen and more coffins. In addition to that came the many who—like Karl's parents—had migrated to the town or America, and who had all, long since, had children and grandchildren. A number too—who didn't have relatives with a house of their own any more but remained attached to the village, even from afar— saw his uncle as a kind of father, and his restaurant as their home back home; and, of course, his uncle also looked after their coffins. He knew: that one there belongs to John, that one to Elianor, even if he'd never met them. (It's even possible that one or other regular customer, though not born in the village, had profited from the goodness of his heart and acquired a coffin.)—Right now, the inn seemed to be closed. No one, not a soul to be seen anywhere—where were they all?— and, now, as the last of the light in the sky vanished, Karl couldn't see his own feet or his hand in front of his nose. Deepest night. The only light was the lantern at the church gate. As if obeying a command, my father walked up to it.

HE FELT HIS WAY TO THE DOOR — the lantern was flattering —
and the door opened before he touched the handle. He entered.
The inside of the Chapel was so bright it dazzled him, and he
closed his eyes. He stumbled for two or three more steps and
then stopped, blind, his hands covering his face. He could feel
a warmth, a heat, that — as he could see when he now carefully opened his eyes and blinked through his fingers — was
coming from a thousand or more candles burning all round
the nave of the church. Candles everywhere, on the floor in
front of him, along the walls, on candelabras the size of wheels
hanging high above him, on the pulpit balustrade and, way
up high, in front of the organ. A sea of light. On the pews sat
men in black clothes, their white faces shimmering in the can-
dlelight. The ancient old men at the front, behind them the old
men, still further back the young and the very young, some
barely older than him. Right in front of him, in the first row,
sat his uncle, massive, with wild hair, and beside him, much
more delicate, his father. How had he managed to overtake
him, unseen and unscathed, though he himself had walked so
quickly, as quickly as humanly possible? — At the rear of the
church he could see the white bonnets of the women. So this
is where they were! They'd been waiting on him! They'd
known, for twelve years they'd known, that he'd come today!
They were all watching, without a movement, wide-eyed, in
silence. Back there, beside a pillar, was his mother, too! Karl
had come in through a side door — there was a tell-tale trail
from the door, a puddle beneath his feet — and was standing
right in front of the altar, on a raised platform full of vases
with flowers. Thistles and alpine roses made of raffia or straw,
as the real ones didn't bloom this early in the year. Everything
was spinning before his eyes; he scouted for a place he could
escape to, behind a pillar, maybe, or out the door again. The

door, though, closed at that very moment, as if by itself, and the snib clicked in the lock. As if someone had turned the key. The altar offered no secret corner, either. It was made of black marble and stood there like a fortress. The whole church was black, indeed, the whole Chapel. The black plaster on the walls glowed. The candles were black — their flames, albeit, shining — the sacred cloths, the bones of martyrs and a whole army of peculiar saints, life-size nearly, that were standing along the walls, holding clubs and picks, halberds and scythes. In front of the altar, at the centre of this church stage, were a table and a chair made of ebony. — Karl was freezing more than ever, he was shivering, trembling, his teeth chattering so much that their clattering could surely be heard in the back row. He felt as if he'd start crying any minute. But the men and women were now smiling. A few girls, way up the back, were literally laughing, even. What, in the name of heaven, was so funny? He was shivering, and soaking wet! — His uncle stood up and stepped up to the altar. He was smiling, too. He raised one hand, and Karl was afraid he was going to hit him. But he simply removed the hat from his head, the jacket-turban, and put both in a basket made of black willow, placed beneath the ebony table. Now everyone was laughing. Karl was blushing crimson. A hat on his head, in a church! And the dripping wet jacket! — But already his uncle had taken his hands and lifted them up, and two men, who had whizzed up from somewhere, and were older still than his uncle, took his shirt off. His shoes. Next his trousers, and underpants. His socks. Next, he was being lifted by four strong hands and — wriggling like a frog — put in a metal tub, full of hot water, that was also, suddenly, on the altar. The two men — his uncle gave them brushes and pieces of soap — scrubbed him from top to bottom. Aggh! He got soap in his eyes right away, of course, though he closed them as tight as he could. It was as if the brushes were trying to skin him. One man washed his head, making it drone, and the other took hold of his penis, slipped the foreskin back, and took the bristles to the glans, whisking them back and forth. But then that, too, was over and done with; his legs now, his feet, his stomach, his back, his behind, arms and legs, and Karl was then being heaved out of the tub, wrapped in hot towels, and rubbed dry. One old man was vigorously rubbing his hair, the other, further down, his stomach and legs. They chuckled and chortled. 'Right!' The towel was removed, and Karl was standing clean, dry, glowing before the congregation. Naked. The men and women looked at him. Far up the back, a few girls had stood up and were straining their necks. But they, too, were looking without ridiculing him. — Their mouths were open, the men's mouths too, the mouths of all the women, and only now did Karl hear them singing. They were all singing. They'd been doing so while he was in the tub with soap in his ears! He'd thought the distant sounds were his own brain cheering! They were singing quietly, like from another world, their voices clear. It was a recurring melody, something like a cannon that, when it seemed to have come to the end in one part of the church, grew in another. The song had words to it — the voices were getting louder — and these, too, were repeated endlessly, the hissing sounds of a language Karl didn't know. Next to him stood the two ancient old men who had washed him, and his uncle. His uncle's eyes were now turned upward, and he was singing like he'd seen the light. Soon, Karl realized he knew the song; the words, even. He must have learnt them while having his bath. He sang along; at first, quietly, cautiously; then, with greater confidence. The song must have been passed down by some forebears or other; by those, perhaps, recalled by the strange statues of saints. — The two ancient

washers stepped down from the altar stage. They were replaced
by two women—gave them, in passing, a pat on the back, and
giggled while, all the while, singing—two very young women
who were also singing, and, in their arms, carrying clothes.
They dressed Karl in dry clothes—now, he did blush: him so
naked, and them so near—so skilfully and quickly, as if they'd
done this countless times. At their age! One was barely fourteen; the other sixteen, at most! They were singing with high,
clear voices, really loudly now, and so Karl, too, belted it out,
as powerfully as he could. (He had a new voice! A bass!)
Underpants, trousers, socks, a shirt, a jacket, his shoes: that
didn't take a minute. The younger of the two, who had blonde
hair and freckles, put a hat in Karl's hand.—He, of course,
didn't put it on. He beamed at the woman, who beamed back.—
The other one, the sixteen-year-old, took him by the hand and
led him to a mirror, set into the altar, that until a moment ago
had been concealed. There he stood—Karl! The new clothes
were like the old ones, except they weren't black. They were
all different shiny colours. The hat, for instance, was red, as
if dyed with wine; the trousers blueberry blue; and the shoes
were made of a leather that changed colour every time he
moved. Chameleon? The socks were yellow. He looked like a
parrot, the only colourful person in the church. He liked what
he saw!—The song reached its climax. Everyone now sang in
loud, enthusiastic fashion, until they all reached the same high
note and then held it for a long time. Soon, it was one note,
all around the church, this one, single note. Vigorous: the
villagers had lungs like bellows. Only after what were minutes did the first give up; had to. The ancient men, the ancient
women, red in the face, their eyes red too, as if about to pop
out of their heads. Then his uncle and my father's father
clapped their mouths shut; both at the same time; both

drenched in sweat. The other old ones. The older young ones and, finally, the very young, too. And then Karl. In the end, only two singers were able to maintain the celebration note: bewilderingly, a toothless old man who had been sitting in the second row, and had now stood up; and the young woman with the freckles who had returned to her seat, far back in the nave. They were competing. They'd focused on one another across all the other heads, and maintained their notes, an octave apart, spurred on by the whole congregation until the old man finally ran out of air, and the woman let another few bars pour from her mouth alone, the sound now all hers as it filled the church finely and clearly. By now, she was so flushed that her freckles had vanished from her cheeks. Then she, too, closed her mouth. The old man, who had lost, croaked, 'Bravo!' Everyone applauded. Karl clapped too.

OF COURSE, he thought that was the end of the ceremony. His uncle, though, raised a hand, and the clapping stopped. Deep silence again. His uncle lifted a black cloth lying on the altar, and from under it took a big — also black — book, a real tome with gilt edging and a ribbon, on the spine of which was Karl's name. *Karl*. 'This is your white book,' his uncle said, so loudly it was as if he were speaking to the whole congregation. 'We call it that because it contains nothing but white pages. In it, you'll note down, from now until you die, each and every day. At length, or in brief — in your own way. Just like all of us here do. In brief, or at length — in our own ways. Even those who can't write add their three Xs every night.' He put the book down, signalled to Karl to sit and then opened the book at the first page, the whiteness of which was so bright that Karl screwed up his eyes. 'No one will ever read what you write before you die,' his uncle said. 'That's something none of us would ever do — read someone else's white book. We'd be forfeiting our salvation. After your death, only then. Then, they certainly will. Then absolutely everyone — including those who can't read, in their own way — will read what your life was like. And be pleased, and cry. And be surprised, and learn. Until then, though, Karl, it is the most secret of all books.' He turned to his nephew, even bent down to him, but continued to speak just as loudly. 'Your first day, today, you will write about before all our eyes. Here. Now.' He gave Karl a sharpened goose quill and pointed to an inkpot. Karl took the quill and dipped it in the pot. He looked at his uncle. 'What's up?' he said, much more quietly now. 'Write what happened. Nothing more, nothing less.' Karl nodded and wrote: '*I am now a man, and today — not for the first time, but for the first time alone, I took the path from my house in the town to the village my father and mother came from.*' He looked up at his uncle. He didn't lift a finger. So Karl continued writing. '*My actual goal was the village church, known as the Black Chapel, though . . .*' — 'Perfect,' his uncle said, taking the quill pen from him. 'That said, if you keep writing like that, so much and in such big letters, your book will soon be full. These pages have to do you for your entire life.' He sprinkled a fine sand across the ink — India ink, of course — then blew it off before closing the book. Everyone immediately got up and crowded towards the exit. They were chatting and babbling and laughing, and no one seemed to give a hang about the Black Chapel being a holy place. Karl was one of the last to leave through the narrow portal. A mild wind. They were all carrying lanterns at the end of long hazel sticks, Chinese lanterns; some carved from sugar beets, too, hideous faces with crooked eyes, warped mouths and grinning teeth. A woman was carrying a lit heart ahead of her; the other side of the lamp had a wolf on it. Karl was given a Chinese lantern on a stick too, a globe made of red paper in which a candle was burning. Four white crosses, one for each point of the compass. He was also carrying his book, which was as heavy as a stone. The front of the procession had long since arrived at the inn. Between it and the church bobbed a few hundred lights. The chatter and laughter rose into the night sky and hung like a cloud over the village. The stars twinkled. Never had Karl seen so many stars in such a deep universe. He messed around with the young men, cracking the same kind of jokes. Further ahead walked his father and mother, hand in hand. That seemed strange, embarrassing, to him. The procession was taking shorter and shorter steps; a tailback had occurred at the gap between the coffins which everyone had to pass to reach the inn. There, everyone was pushing and shoving—Karl now, too—pressed tight against one another, laughing and screeching. The ones behind him were crushing him to death, nearly—a horde of crowing girls—while he was stuck to the back of a hefty man. He could hardly breathe and, soon, was thrown against the coffins so violently that they teetered over him, as if about to crash down on top of him. In front of him, his coffin: he recognized it right away, though the red box, by the light of the Chinese lanterns—everyone was holding them above their heads—looked more massive than it usually did. 'My coffin is outside the blacksmith's shop,' the woman with the freckles said, behind him. He would have recognized her voice among thousands of others though she hadn't said a single word to him. Her singing! She was pushed against him—her breast, her stomach, her legs— and had her mouth so close to his ear that he could feel her breath. 'We've only three coffins left now. My mother's, my brother's and mine. My father's we needed last week.' She breathed into Karl's ear; her breath was hot. 'But our coffins are still the tidiest pile in the whole village. My father used a spirit level to align them. Flush left, flush right. I know how to do that, too.' — The left side of Karl's face was dragged along the coffin boards like across sandpaper. (Once, his ear got caught on the edge of a coffin, and he yelled out, unheard. The breath, still at his other ear.) — Where were the coffins of his father and of his mother? — Finally, the coffin bottleneck was behind them and they reached the inn.

IT WAS A PROPER HALL, much bigger than Karl remembered. Bright, with long tables at which the guests were seated. Garlands criss-crossing the room, high above their heads. They, too, either black or white. The men had taken off their jackets and were in their shirts — the sleeves rolled up, here and there — and the women had removed their bonnets and loosened their bodices. Many had undone their buns, and their hair now flowed down their backs. Karl was still the only one in colourful clothes, but the others' faces were now so animated that they had colourful glows. Their noses red, their cheeks flushed. A woman wearing glasses that looked as if she'd made them herself, using wire and plain glass, took Karl by the hand and pulled him to a table that took up the full length of the rear wall. Fire-brigade flags; cups; winners' certificates, framed, from cattle exhibitions. Here, too, all the seats were taken. All apart from two: the one for the glasses woman, and Karl's. This was the seat of honour, at the centre of the table, so that Karl could see the whole room and could be seen by everyone; and it was garlanded with lobelia. There was a scent from the flowers; he'd never smelt anything like it. Nor did he know what to do with the book — no one came to help; they all seemed curious to see how he'd solve the problem—so in the end he sat on it. He sat there: enthroned like a king; or like a hunter in his raised hide. Everyone clapped; he'd found the correct solution. The woman with the glasses—like everyone else at the table, barely older than him—sat down beside him. 'I am your maid of honour,' she said. 'My name is Hildi. And that's Else.' Else was sitting on his other side; she was chubby, and already had huge breasts. She beamed at him.—The one with the freckles was sitting off to the side, away down the table. At the same table, at least.— Women were coming from the kitchen—aunts and cousins; he still knew the name of one: Zelda—and serving steaming-hot bowls of bacon, beans and potatoes. The men of the family running the inn—also cousins or uncles—were filling the glasses with a wine that was, indeed, the same colour as his hat. Karl gobbled his food down so quickly that Zelda hadn't moved on and so could refill his plate. 'The town ones,' she said, 'always need a second helping.' Karl looked up at her, gratefully. He was dying of thirst, too, though—and so emptied his glass in a oner. It was his first time ever, the first time he'd drunk wine, and he liked it. He held his glass out to a cousin who was maybe also an uncle. The boy filled it again, and Karl emptied it as quickly. And, of course, was poured yet another. Hildi and Else raised their glasses to him. Yes, he had to get up—slump from his book to the floor—and toast the whole room. A few hundred glasses stretched in his direction and from as many throats '*Prost*' was roared, the sound resembling the bark of new-born dragons. He made a similar sound, emptied his glass, and climbed back onto the throne. Soon, he was in a great mood, matching that of everyone around him: they were all speaking at the same time, and as loudly as they possibly could. They wanted to be understood, but not necessarily understand what the others were saying. Karl was roaring into the general din, too — with the boom of his newly acquired bass — and telling Else, who was speaking across him to Hildi, that he was a far better footballer than his brother, and that a horse-drawn tram operated between the station and the lake. The others were shouting the names of German armoured cruisers to one another — *Prince Bismarck*, *Scharnhorst*, *Victoria Louise* — and the women were giggling about dresses from Paris, that you could see the top of the breasts, that they'd never wear anything like that, but would actually like to, once, at least. — Later, the tables were pushed together. A band — accordion, double bass, some kind of mandolin — climbed onto a high platform in a corner of the hall. Immediately, the floor was full of dancers. Karl jumped up, too — with Hildi. He hopped and he twirled; and Hildi jumped about like a filly. Soon Else turned up and replaced Hildi, who laughed and returned to her seat though not a single woman was now sitting. The women had surrounded the dance floor. They all had their eyes on Karl. Each and every one of them, it turned out, wanted to dance with him, literally every one, the old and really old women too, and so he ended up waltzing with dancers who hadn't a tooth in their heads and who used him as a zimmer. At one point, even with a centenarian, for whom the tiniest of steps were huge jumps. She beamed with happiness, and Karl thought it was great, too. Suddenly, his mother was in his arms. after an English waltz, the musicians were packing away their instruments, she half stood up, blushing deeply, as if about to ask for a last dance, but then sat down again. Karl was now seated again, too, and soon blustering with the lads. They spoke about the Panama Canal as if they'd been present at the opening; and about the Battle of the Marne. Karl told them about a German (of course) aviator called Ölerich who had set a new world altitude record by flying at a height of more than 8,000 metres. He was speaking only for the benefit of the women with the freckles, who was, indeed, listening attentively, from a distance. By now, he was completely thrilled by everything; and everything was spinning round him. He no longer knew: was it him who was speaking, at the moment; or, more likely, another man at the table? Everyone was speaking for everyone else. — At some point, he looked up; perhaps because the general din had quietened, after all. The room was empty. An uncle and two female cousins were clearing the tables, taking away the glasses and carafes. They were casting gigantic shadows on the walls — only a few lamps were burning, now — and crumpling the paper tablecloths with their paws. It sounded like cannon fire. The room looked wasted: bottles knocked over, bits of broken glass, drooping garlands. Karl stared, as if through opal glass, at a cousin's behind as she crawled under a table. Then, when it was his table's turn, he tried to get up. He took a lurch. He managed, at least, to save a lobelia — as the glasses were whisked away; the carafes, too; and the tablecloths went into a basket — that was more fragrant than ever. He smelt and smelt at it, then put it in one of his trouser pockets. Not a soul at a table any more. Opposite him, just, a young man with whom, hours before, he'd discussed the strengths and weaknesses of the Ford T, was hanging over the arm of his chair, his mouth open and snoring. The landlord tipped him onto the floor but he didn't wake up. Only when Karl shook him did he open one eye, clap his mouth shut and struggle to his feet. It was then he who led Karl — each holding on to the other — into an extension of the inn. The barn, probably; a large room, in any case. It was pitch dark and smelt of hay. The two of them clowned around a bit until, simultaneously, several voices cursed in the darkness. It's possible, even, a shoe flew through the air; Karl felt a blast of air, and something clattered to the ground behind him. He fell into the hay; wherever. To his right and left snored sleepers. Whether there were female sleepers in the barn, too, he didn't know; he'd yet to hear a sleeping woman. He couldn't imagine women making such a racket, though; that coarse. — He'd just slipped into that realm between waking and sleep — shimmering images, distant sounds, confused voices — when he felt a breath on his cheek, a body at his side. A woman. 'Psst!' — barely audible in his ear. Lips were kissing his lips, and soon — the shock, at first, had made his stiffen — he was kissing back. He could smell the woman's scent; it reminded him of something familiar. He grunted, and a hand went over his mouth. So he was quiet again. His female visitor's other hand, and soon the original hand too, wandered over him. His hands, too — while their lips continued to kiss — went wherever they were welcome. They were welcome everywhere. Now, it was the woman who sighed, quietly, without removing her lips from Karl's. Once, perhaps because Karl had moved vigorously, one of his sleeping neighbours gasped as if he were about to wake, and twisted and turned, causing the female visitor, now partly on top of Karl, to freeze. Karl was stiff as a board, too. When the snoring resumed, her lips became softer again, and Karl's too. — Suddenly, without a hint of a farewell, she was gone. Karl sat up, stared into the darkness and flailed about. Nothing. No one. Not a whiff or waft to indicate someone fleeing through the hay. Who had been the tender guest? How had she known where he was lying? — Karl fell asleep so quickly that he dreamt what happened next, as if there hadn't been a parting. Perhaps it had been a dream from the start. — When he woke, bright light shone through the cracks in the wooden walls. Above them, high above, a straw roof. He raised his head. Indeed: hay from one wall to the other. He was alone. Not a soul, not even depressions in the hay where they'd been sleeping. Outside, on the other hand, he could hear voices. A confusion of voices. So he got up—his head booming, his throat dry as dust—flicked the blades of grass from his jacket, put on his hat, put the leather sack over his shoulder, lifted his book and went outside. A slanting morning sun. He blinked. At the edge of a fountain, a hollowed-out tree trunk, sat his father and mother. They beamed at him. He plunged his head in the trough. Then drank so greedily you'd have thought he wanted to drain the source.—The square that led up to the fortress-like houses, right at at the top, was full of people. They were wearing coarse heavy jackets, and heavy coats, all of the same material, and besieging market stalls where black salsifies were piled in pyramids. Potatoes, clay still sticking to them. Murky-coloured beetroot. But leather bags too, and cast-iron pans. Those candles Karl had seen in the church. Black and white currants. As he walked around the stalls—his parents following him—he recognized many of the people visiting the market. Nearly all of them. They'd been at his celebration yesterday. Now, however, they weren't bothering with him. One of his aunts, for instance, was talking away to the old man who'd held the last note for so long; and neither heard him say hello. An uncle and a cousin passed him without interrupting their conversation. One of the ancient old washers ran into him, even, yet appeared not to recognize him. Else was standing at a table full of wriggling eels—did they eat those? She didn't respond, either. Hildi, a few stalls further, was selling grey bulbs; gentian roots perhaps. Karl waved to her and wasn't sure whether she winked at him; or was it the sun, reflecting on her glasses? Zelda, too—his cousin—walked past, indifferent.—Karl was walking, his feet wide apart, along the lane that was like a wave of cobbles, and yet he still felt sea-sick. He was better, this time, at avoiding the mules' puddles. The blacksmith's, at the end of the lane, was a gorge of soot and grime. Its three coffins were, indeed, especially carefully aligned. Which one was that of the woman with the freckles? Karl touched one of the coffins so quickly, so casually, that his parents didn't spot it. He wasn't sure if he'd got the right one, but this coffin, of an almost-white wood, seemed more graceful than the other two. Beyond the village, the path led to the four chalk rocks that jutted into the sky like fingers. To the turn in the path. Karl turned back, one last time. Outside the blacksmith's now stood a figure that, when he waved, raised a hand and vanished into the house. The barns and houses of the village were shining black. The church weathercock was gleaming. Karl, obviously, had to find his way back alone, too: his father and mother were letting him walk ahead. So he headed straight for the sun — it was its task to show him the way — and immediately came across the ravine where he'd battled with thunder and lightning. Now, in the morning light, the mosses and stones were bright and friendly. He took the path with the glimmering stones, past the ancient stone pines, where no birds were perched any more. He was running, almost, but his parents remained on his heels. Soon, the sun was directly above him; and when he got to the tree stump, the place for his rest, his shadow was pointing the way, already. Again, he was hungry; again, he sat down. In the leather sack were, again, some bread, some cheese and some cider. Someone had filled it. 'Want some, Father? You, Mother?' Both shook their heads. — Across the snowfield, past the quarry, the track with the blackberry twines, beneath the firs, between the oaks and the beeches: Karl was now walking so quickly that his parents fell behind, after all. Nonetheless, the broad roadway in the lowest section of the forest was already in shadow; the Old Customs inn and the redoubts weren't in the light, either. But when Karl turned into his street, the evening light was still gilding his house. Familiar colours—after so much ancestral black—everywhere he looked; his clothes too—which yesterday had seemed like feathers—were back to normal. Even his shoes—so, chameleons, after all—were hard to tell apart from the cobbles. Karl waited outside the door until his parents turned up, soaked with sweat and fighting for breath. 'Now, *you* are the strong one,' his father panted. His mother was wheezing too much to be able to say anything, and tried to run her fingers through Karl's hair. He dodged her and ran up the stairs, into the apartment. Felix was at the kitchen table, smirking. 'My maids of honour were called Berta and Olga,' he said. 'Great dames.' Karl stuck his tongue out at him, bolted into the room they shared, locked the door, heaved his book up onto the wardrobe—for the first time he noticed that a similar one lay there already: Felix' white book— and opened the window. He leant out. A gentle wind, stirring dust here and there. A man with a long shadow waiting beside a plane tree, the shadow of which reached the end of the street where a dog and its shadow sniffed around it. Karl thought of the woman who'd visited him at night. He was now sure it had been the one with the freckles. Anyone else would have been the wrong one. Her kisses! He took the lobelia from his pocket—it looked terrible, shrivelled—and smelt it. He inhaled the scent so deeply that the flower head got stuck in his nostril, and caused a really big sneeze. Suddenly, he needed to pee, too, like never before in his life. He bolted to the door, shook it—until Felix shouted, 'Key, you fool!'—flew down the corridor, out of the apartment, and, in a single leap, down all the steps of the staircase. Still running—sneezing a final time, too—he tore down his trousers. But it wasn't a pee he needed. Something white shot out of him, once, twice, across the loo, and as far as the window. He stood there, blind, forgetting to breathe, his brain hammering. Was he sick? Dying? When he got his breath back, and could see again, he took out his hanky and wiped the walls and window. It was a miracle he hadn't splattered the ceiling. He buttoned up his trousers, flushed the toilet and went back to the apartment. Felix, still sitting in the kitchen, grinned. This time, Karl didn't lock the door. He opened the window. A cool air. The man on the street below pulled the lead so firmly that the dog gave up and trotted off behind him. Karl, my father, watched them go. When he made to whisper the name of the woman with the freckles, he realized he didn't know what she was called.

EVERY SON IS CONVINCED that his father has never slept with a woman; barely with the one who then became his mother; or, at the outside, on that one occasion. And not, in any case, with any others. A fallacy, of course. Always. In the case of my father, however, that's how it was. Exactly how it was. The woman with the freckles was the first, with whom he fell in love; with whom, however, he did not sleep. Whom, with all his heart, he wanted to see again, and yet that passion remained imprisoned in his head. (He did, in fact, see her again; once; fifty years later.) And, of course, the pain of this first parting passed; he was young, there were other women. A Regula he glowed at from a distance. A Marie-Jo he fetched from school and accompanied home, prattling frantically; once, they even went to a funfair and ate gingerbread and discussed the Revolution in Russia. Marie-Jo was against, and my father wasn't quite sure. (Marie-Jo later became a doctor, married a doctor and killed herself by injecting morphine on the evening of the day her husband had died in the morning.) A Stephanie explained the stars in the sky to him—the Plough, the Little Bear, Venus—and first he stared up into the universe; then he squeezed her against him. She squeezed back for a minute or two, then said with a croaky voice that if they continued like that, the two of them, it would end up being beastly. She ran off. (She turned, not even two months later, to his best friend and let things turn uninhibitedly beastly.) A Monika with whom he went for a walk in the forest and felt mature and adult when she, on one occasion, suddenly had to go and hunkered behind a bush. He understood that women, too, are pestered by their bowels; and not only men. (Monika, with another partner, became a successful competitive dancer and took fourth place at the *Grand Tournoi de Danse de Monte Carlo*.) With a Susanne he even lay down once—(both) believing her parents and brothers and sisters were up Mt Säntis—without any clothes on, on a bed full of teddy bears. Susanne was naked, too. They looked at one another, breathlessly thrilled by what they were seeing. They almost touched, her mouth trembling already over his. But then there was a clattering sound on the ground floor: the wanderers were back, hours early. It had been raining even at the foot of Mt Säntis, and the summit had been wrapped in thick clouds. My father had never dressed so quickly, and Susanne was back in her clothes even faster. (She then married a man from an exotic country, from Celebes or Sumatra, and lived barefoot and with a red dot on her forehead in his homeland which, by the time he died, had also become hers.) By now, my father was a student; he studied Romance languages and their literatures, and got into those farces from the Middle Ages in which fat monks lie with good-humoured nuns, and abbesses bestride bishops

who stop over on their pilgrimage to Santiago de Compostela.
Yes, all along the Way of St James, the pious pilgrims wal-
lowed together, seven to a bed; and many a pilgrim turned—
though her legs had already done six hundred Spanish miles,
and had as many ahead of them again—from her left-hand
neighbour in the bed to her right-hand one, who, for his part,
had just caused the heart of a novice—she'd rejoiced so much
that all the other salvation-seekers paused in their search for
their own salvation—to merge with her Lord and Saviour.—
The clever Abaelardus, with whose rebellious nature he thought
he'd a lot in common, was my father's favourite; and, of course,
he was delighted that Abelard first knew his Héloise, in the
biblical sense, right behind the high altar of his religious
order's church. A place where one didn't think to look, of
course; but a sacrilege, too, of which my father, perhaps even
Abelard, approved. The fact that, and way in which, Héloise's
uncle's henchmen harassed Abelard—they castrated him—
appealed to my father less. If he imagined too hard how—
roaring with laughter—they waved the streaming-with-blood
penis back and forth before Abelard's eyes, he'd curl up in
pain, almost like the latter. He flipped the book shut. That was
the advantage of books: he could close them if the life within
them got too much for him. He'd then begin another and read,
for instance, about that chaste nun who never went to the loo
and, begging for release, slid up to her god on her knees and
shat so many hard stones that in the end she was able to build
a chapel.—My father began a collection of such magnificent
stories; unearthed dusty prints in the few second-hand book-
shops in town; and so, when he lived in Paris for a year—in
the Twenties—he thought he was in paradise. Every second
shop offered old books for sale, at least on the *rive gauche*, that
therefore also became his hunting ground. He'd gone to Paris

because everyone has to have lived in Paris at least once; and
because he was on the heels of a woman, a real woman, made
of flesh and blood. Hélène was her name, she was a few years
older than him — twenty-seven or twenty-eight, to be blunt —
and a teacher of French everyday speech at the university
where he was a student. She was his teacher. That said, everyday speech didn't interest him especially — more moved, as he
was, by the idioms of the Early and High Middle Ages; or
rather, it interested him only if he got to speak it with her. He
did exactly that after once beginning a conversation with her,
or she did so with him, for she asked him for a light when,
coincidence or not, they left the lecture theatre side by side as
they headed out into the corridor. (That was near the end of
the semester; he'd never have had the courage to ask *her* for a
match.) She smoked like a chimney, cigarettes made with a
yellow corn paper and a black tobacco that somebody — a
fiancé, who was waiting for her? — sent from Paris, and that
she puffed away one after the other. She had yellow fingers,
and my father was someone who liked women with nicotine-
stained hands. He fell in love for what — after the woman with
the freckles — was the second time, deeply and passionately. He
and Hélène were soon meeting every day in a stand-up cafe
near the university, in the breaks, for — alongside her teaching
contract — Hélène was studying the literature of German
Romanticism with the same ardour that my father showed
when tracing medieval nuns and monks. She spoke German
very well, with a slight accent, and knew Eduard Mörike's
Nolten the Painter by heart. It was her favourite book, though
her advisor told her again and again that Mörike was a poet
of the Biedermeier period, not a Romantic, and so didn't con-
cern her in the least. She didn't care, just as she didn't care
about so many things — for instance, whether many, or just a

few, students attended her courses—and that, too, was something she'd in common with my father. He contradicted his teachers often and vehemently, and could never understand why they didn't appreciate that. Bullshit was bullshit, and it had to be possible to say so. Hélène and he went for walks in the city park, and in the Bois des Rossignols (normally the preserve of the gays). They walked hand in hand, and sometimes he pressed her against a tree and kissed her. She kissed him back, very much so, but also told him about a sorrow, about a man who, each time she spoke about him, seemed to grow bigger and more powerful, a sensual monster, for whom she'd fallen, head over heels, and with heart and soul, and who, without any warning or justification, had left her, not for another woman, even. He was simply—his words—fed up with her. In the grey light of dawn, he'd got out of their bed and into his trousers, without a word, and gone. He'd left the door open. He *wasn't* the one sending the cigarettes; a girlfriend from her first years at university, and now the assistant of a big fish at the Collège de France, arranged those. Hélène always knew the latest gossip from back home. That, as of late, Pétain, turning grey gracefully, was letting a barely twenty-year-old lover have his marshal's baton; or that Anatole France possessed so much wisdom of age that now he only spoke in capital letters. That Paul Claudel wanted to convert André Gide to the true faith. Conversely, she did not believe that, in her century, *one* single significant picture had been painted; and mocked Kandinsky, who considered his blots and scrawls to be art. She preferred Watteau and Fragonard; at most she'd have admitted Corot, and Renoir. My father, who actually felt differently, nodded anyway.—On one occasion, they were lying—him, with his trousers down at his knees; her, with her dress up at her navel—on the couch in

her room—gentleman visitors were forbidden—and were
rolling around on top of one another. Kissing, biting and tug-
ging at one another's underwear. Somehow it didn't come to
anything and, in the end, they lay, wet, next to one another,
not daring to look at one another.—What had happened to
Hélène in Paris with the beloved monster, she now did to my
father. One day, suddenly, she was gone. A slip of paper with
a laconic greeting lay on his desk. He gulped, gave the walls
a few kicks, threw a couple of books across the room and,
with new fervour, threw himself into his nuns and monks. A
few weeks later, he followed her, moneyless, or almost, to Paris.
He didn't know where she lived, roamed restlessly through all
the reading rooms of all the libraries and scoured every cafe in
the *quartier latin*. In between, he killed time at the *bouquinistes*
along the Seine and, with money he didn't have, bought one
book after another. That is, he begged his Papa and Mama
again and again for a new advance, and they sent him the
money—along with loving letters full of concerned under-
tones—then lived, even more than before, off chicory coffee,
two-day-old bread and fried potatoes done without lard. Not
that my father was living it up. He'd rented one of those holes
beneath the roof in the Rue du Bac, whose only light came
through slanting windows set into the tiles. He slept on a mattress on the floor, and fetched water in a jug from downstairs.
A table, a chair. His clothes on hangers on a line tied across
the room. No toilet; he had to use a cafe opposite. Otherwise:
books. They piled up everywhere, every day a few more, for
my father had discovered an antiquarian bookseller in Rue de
Buci, who had the most wonderful books on sale at reasonably affordable prices because all of his offers had a snag of
some kind. You only had to spot the catch. The Complete
Voltaire in twenty-eight volumes, for instance, was missing

Vol. XXIII. In the case of Diderot's *Encyclopédie*—a miracle of a work that had my father trembling—the volumes with the illustrations had gone astray. Rousseau's *Nouvelle Héloïse*—it, too, a first edition—was so foxed that the title page was barely legible, and he'd to compare the actual text with a cheap softcover version in order to understand it. The illustrations had been cut out of a beautiful edition of Banville's poems.— Above all, though, my father was aided by the crisis facing the French franc—its value was dropping, dramatically, by the hour—and by the complicity of the single employee in the bookshop. He, you see, a Monsieur Lefèbre, was in a simmering conflict with his boss, Monsieur Eschwiller, a typical Parisian whose forefathers were from Alsace. Why Monsieur Lefèbre liked Monsieur Eschwiller so little didn't ever become entirely clear to my father; Monsieur Lefèbre settled for vague hints; and Monsieur Eschwiller, hardly ever in the shop, was maybe not at all aware of the conflict, and all its drama. It was to do with derogatory remarks—'*Monsieur Lefèbre, vous êtes bête comme vos pieds!*'—and with one of Monsieur Eschwiller's daughters whom Monsieur Lefèbre wanted to marry either at any price or not under any circumstances. Difficult to say, which; Monsieur Lefèbre, at any rate, didn't seem to have lost his senses. There was something more of a rabbit about him, forced to wear a stiff collar and a tie. His revenge on Monsieur Eschwiller was to sell his books to my father at precisely the price his boss had indicated on the back cover. Only, with inflation racing, these prices became more and more absurd every day. And so my father acquired a 1712 edition of Marguerite d'Angoulême's *Heptaméron*—later, thirty years later, he translated the book, using precisely this edition—for a few notes; and Baudelaire's translations of the works of Edgar Allan Poe almost for free; and neither Monsieur Lefèbre nor

my father revealed they were aware of any irregularity. '*Merci,
Monsieur*. Do us the honour again soon.' — '*Au revoir, Monsieur
Lefèbre*. I wish you a pleasant evening.' No wonder my father
tapped his father and mother more and more frequently, by
turns, for the very much modest amounts they transferred
became — when he changed them at the Banque de Paris
counter on Boulevard St-Germain, and then ran, at the double, to the bookshop on Rue de Buci — a small fortune. At any
rate, by the end of the year, he'd bought himself a precious
library, if one consisting of books without their original cov-
ers or of not-quite-complete complete editions. The books, by
now, were forming walls around his mattress, reaching up to
the slanting roof tiles and proliferating out into the corridor. —
Also at the end of the year, shortly before Christmas, my
father — with a first edition of Jules Vernes' *Michel Strogoff*
under his arm, the title page of which contained the hand-
written dedication '*A mon cher Emile, ton oncle Jules*'; and which
had cost my father five francs — was going down the Boule-
vard Saint-Michel when, suddenly, he was standing in front
of Hélène. She'd a red, blocked nose, and was at least as taken
aback as him. Nothing less than startled. She told him her
address. She was living very close, in Rue Bonaparte, had lived
above it the whole time. She shopped at the same greengrocer
as my father, and even knew Monsieur Lefèbre. (He didn't
offer her inflation prices, though.) My father invited her for a
coffee but she didn't want to go. She didn't want to go for a
meal with him on one of the feast-day evenings, either. She
didn't want to go for a meal with him at all. Ever. 'Salut!' She
walked on, in a long grey coat and a fur cap, beneath which
her black hair hung to her shoulders. — My father laid siege to
the apartment well into spring, climbed the steep staircase to
her door several times a day, knocked and waited, knocked

again and pressed his ear to the wood, and, on one or other occasion, could probably hear a rustling, or someone breathing.
He sat for hours in the cafe at her corner; went in the morning, at noon and in the evening to the greengrocer they had in
common; and wrote her glowing letters. Once, he left a bouquet of roses outside her door; once, a rare edition of Diderot's
Bijoux indiscrets. Nothing, not ever, not a single time did he
meet her, with the result that, in the end, the suspicion took
root that, back then, she'd moved out that same day, or given
him a false address, even. — In spring — a first warm sun, the
swallows were back — my father walked through the Jardin
du Luxembourg. Hélène was sitting on a bench, enjoying the
sun through closed eyes. When he stopped in front of her and
said 'Hélène!', she jumped up like a fury. She now had her eyes
open — hellfire glowing in them — and shouted that she'd had
enough of this carry-on; and that my father should buzz off
once and for all — right away, at the very latest — otherwise,
there was going to be an accident. She was shaking with anger,
Hélène. Walkers were gathering round her and my father, such
that the latter stammered 'But . . . I . . . Hélène . . .' turned,
and — in as composed a manner as he could muster — headed
towards the park exit. He was already a dozen or so yards
away when he noticed he'd not raised his hat. So he took it off;
also because he'd to wipe the sweat from his brow. The group
of onlookers gawped at him, and Hélène, in the far distance
already, hurried off, her skirts swaying, and disappeared
behind a box hedge. My father put his hat back on, went to his
dugout in Rue du Bac, packed all his books into boxes —
except, of course, his white book which he never let out of his
sight — and charged the Paris branch of Danzas with sending
them back to his homeland. How he was going to pay the
transportation costs he didn't know. (He was then in debt to

them for almost six months, and then tapped Felix for the money when Danzas threatened to prosecute him—Felix, who promised to say not a word to their parents, and whom he owed the money right up to his—that is, Felix's—death.) He'd had enough, in any case, of this Paris where it always rained, a terrible rain swept through the streets, and where—although he'd always used the same cafe and regularly attended the lectures of Joseph Bédiers—he'd not made a single friend, never mind found a girlfriend. The ground had always—hardly would he have exchanged a few friendly words with them—swallowed them up, it seemed. Monsieur Lefèbre was thus actually the only person with whom he had any kind of friendship, and so my father, one mild May morning, went to the second-hand bookshop on Rue de Buci a final time to say goodbye. Not Monsieur Lefèbre, but Monsieur Eschwiller, was at the till, though, and he snarled—when my father asked him to convey warm regards to Monsieur Lefèbre—that he'd sacked the latter today, or that his daughter had married him yesterday. Something along those lines, anyway. Apart from '*Ah, Monsieur Lefèbre, ah, ah, celui-là!*', my father understood not a word. He nodded and left.—At home, in the town, he returned to the university—every single person was still sitting in the same place, as if the uni were the castle in *Sleeping Beauty*—and became, as quickly as at all possible, a *Doctor philosophiae*. His doctoral thesis—*Popular similes of the type 'rouge comme le coq'*— gained him a *magna cum laude* and the attention of his professor who, at that very moment, needed a new assistant. The old one, though still young, had collapsed to dust and been declared unfit for work though he'd never actually worked. And so my father took his seat at the desk in the antechamber of the Romanic Department; answered—like his predecessor—the questions of first-year students; and checked—more as a formality—the bags, poly-bags and folders of anyone leaving the department. He didn't enjoy his work, but was paid a salary and now lived in his own three-room apartment. Barely room for him and his books. The apartment was directly beneath that of his parents, whom he heard, from time to time, shuffling back and forth. (Felix no longer lived at home. He'd become a pastor in a small parish in the Canton of Basel-Land, where he awaited greater tasks.) He began work on his habilitation—perhaps he'd complete it in time to replace his boss, a Herr Tappolet—and chose as his topic his nuns and monks. The editions of the farces he uncovered piled up on his desk; and many a first-year, while his folder was supposedly being checked, got to hear a juicy précis of what his male and female heroes had got up to that day. Often, a dozen students would gather round him, giggling.—He did, however, know a few real women, a Renate, a Sophie and a Paula. He went to concerts with them, to the Philharmonic, and a few times to the Young Orchestra. The musicians in the latter looked like children in tails and evening dresses, and played pieces by composers no one had ever heard of. Armand Hiebner, Conrad Beck, Béla Bartók, Igor Stravinsky, whom my father did know; as did Renate and Sophie but not Paula. That said, he liked most of all to take his women to the cinemas that were now opening. A bright screen, a dark room and in one corner a pianist who bowed at the end. Whenever Charlie Chaplin put the head of the idiotic, gigantic policeman in a gas lamp, he and Paula and Sophie and Renate roared with laughter, grabbing hold of one another; and with tears in their eyes. *Battleship Potemkin* he saw eight times: three times with Renate; twice with Sophie; once with Paula—who thought the film boring; and twice alone. When the sailors, shaking with rage, refused to give an inch, he held his breath.—Once, he had

Sophie back to his flat; she'd made sweet dumplings, and he'd opened two bottles of Beaujolais. They'd had plenty to drink, drinking until late at night, so late, indeed, that Sophie began to wonder whether she should surrender to Karl, so funny with his swagger. (From a good background, she didn't ever do so casually.) My father, caused considerable doubts by the same question in reverse, put her fur round her shoulders in the middle of a discussion about Nietzsche—to do with why the latter had kissed a horse in Turin, and how such a thing could be reconciled with the concept of the *Übermensch*—and offered to accompany her home. It was now three a.m. She got up immediately, of course, though she'd frozen with astonishment. She kissed him passionately, then went to the door with such determination that it was impossible to turn back. Standing on the pavement outside the house—it was pitch dark, the streetlights not being lit at this hour—was my father's mother, sweeping the leaves that had fallen from the plane trees up into a pile. She pretended not to see the loving couple; and Sophie and Karl did the same.—After that, my father didn't take any more women home with him, though he'd soon be over thirty. And so Clara Molinari, whom he carried over the threshold of his apartment, and who now shared his surname, was, indeed, the first woman, with whom he not only fell in love but also slept.

IT WAS A WONDERFUL NIGHT. My father and Clara kissed as if time didn't exist; and, when my father got up to go to the window to smoke a cigarette, the sun was already shining onto the trunks of the plane trees. The dust in the street was glowing like gold. A bird landed on the window ledge, looked at my father, its head at a slant, and flew off again, chirping. The air was fresh. My father, who hadn't slept for a single minute and was wide awake, put his trousers on. 'Coffee, Clara?' Clara emitted a blissful sound, curled up beneath the cover, and was immediately asleep. — She and my father made love all the following night, too; and the one after that; and the one after that. The nightingales sang — Clara and my father kissed — and, when the larks took over, the two of them were still lying, wrapped up in one another. The days were hardly any different. My father hugged Clara wherever he met her; and she caressed the back of his neck as he read his post. He would catch her at the bathroom door when she was about to pluck her eyebrows; or, up in the attic, would shoot out from behind the wet sheets hung up on long ropes — as if he were a ghost — making Clara drop the washing basket with fright or joy. Or he would creep up to her in the kitchen when she was at the stove, preparing a sauce for the spaghetti. Tomatoes, herbs, garlic: her Italian aunts had taught her to cook. He'd put his arms round her, from behind, and she'd threaten him with a raised spoon, 'I'm cooking, Karl!' — not that it helped her any, 'I'm cooking too!' my father would whisper into her ear, and soon they'd be on the bed again, licking every patch of skin their tongues could reach. — On the stove, in the pan, the sauce would be burning. — It didn't bother them that they lived on the ground floor, and that the window was open so that anyone passing could hear their cries of joy. (On one occasion, my father's Mama was returning from the shops, and her son let out a roar — the flames of hell, you'd have thought, were shooting out of him — just as she passed their window. She got such a fright that her bag slipped from her hand, and potatoes, apples and a few carrots rolled around in the dust. A piece of cheese. As she picked everything up again, the racket above her became less noisy and, eventually, subsided altogether.) On another occasion, my father was so impatient — or was he in the mood, for once, to show his nuns and monks what he was capable of? — that, there and then, he pulled Clara, cleaning the window in their library, down to the carpet, a scratchy mat made of stubble-like reeds that lay between the high walls of books. She landed on her back, my father over her; and she parted her legs — was it lust? or pain? — so dramatically that the books tumbled down, burying her and my father. They were roaring, meanwhile, in the greatest of ecstasies — in those times of burning passion, that could take a matter of seconds, just — and wouldn't have been surprised if the whole house had collapsed around them. They huffed and puffed regardless, buried beneath the Complete Works of Voltaire and French peasant farces, and were still laughing when they'd tunnelled their way back out into daylight. Clara stood up. Her behind was ripped to shreds, and so my father slid over on his knees to kiss her wounds until Clara, ruffling his hair, said, 'Right, that's enough!' He beamed up at her. He was happy in a way he'd never been before. — A few weeks later, they moved into a different apartment. My father's father, you see, had acquired the habit of bringing them a biblical quotation every evening that he'd noted on a piece of paper; and my father's mother, at any time of day, would look in the window and ask if they needed anything from the market. Above all, however, Clara's sister, Nina, had just got married; and, with her husband, Rüdiger, a young public prosecutor at the juvenile court, was now building a house. Fellow residents were required, and that — of course — could only be Clara and my father. When they moved in, the scaffolding hadn't yet been taken down. The house was located at the furthest edge of town, or to be more precise, it had raced ahead of the town, and rose like a lonely outpost from among fields of crops, meadows full of poppies and cherry trees. A narrow drive that came to an end at the back corner of the garden fence. It was, even if surrounded by ringing cowbells, anything but rural. The architect was a pupil of Walter Gropius — Rüdiger loved New Objectivity — and, with this project, hoped to prove himself to his teacher. It was his first commission. And so, making no compromises, even with the door handles and the letterboxes, he built a cube of exposed concrete and glass, so much glass, in fact, that the house looked like a gigantic aquarium, especially at night, when, even from a distance, the residents could be seen swimming around in it. (Curtains were taboo. A few months later, however, Clara had curtain rails installed, and simply put up with the architect — he checked almost daily that things were as they should be — raging round the rooms, calling her square and reactionary.) She and my father were again living on the ground floor. Nina and Rüdiger were on the first. (The second floor consisted of a roof terrace and two small one-room flats that, for the moment, remained empty. On the flat roof was a radio aerial, as tall as a ship mast, which enabled my father to listen to mysterious stations like BBC London and Radio Honolulu.) — Nina had hoped Clara would help to finance the house. (Both sisters had married men without means.) Which is to say: she and Clara had inherited money when their father — their mother was already four years dead — died on 26 October 1929. It was a Saturday morning, and he was reading the newspaper report on Black Friday. He fell, lifeless, from his chair. All his securities, which, even the previous evening, had made him a rich man, were now worthless. There was an inheritance, nonetheless. The railway stocks, and those of Ciba Chemicals, did bring in some money; very much so; and there was also a piece of ground, far beyond the protective forest — that is, the very land on which the new house was now situated; a

holiday chalet in Zweisimmen; and a high-quality, almost contemporary, Canaletto reproduction that a Belgian collector
bought, who, two days before the Crash, with considerable
foresight, had got rid of all his securities and now, with his
pockets full of money, was chasing the paintings owned by
the victims of the Crash. He got the fake Canaletto for half its
value, but even this half was a considerable sum. Each sister
got something like one hundred and fifty thousand Swiss
francs. For Nina—six years younger than her sister—it represented a fortune, whereas Clara—even when she got her
hands on the inheritance with which she hadn't reckoned—
remained badly hit by the Crash. That was her father's legacy.
She had found him, on his back, the newspaper with the terrible news crushed in one hand, his motionless eyes wide
open. Seated at the desk for nights on end, *she* had totted up
the losses; practically given away the villa because she couldn't
pay the mortgage; and given away the car. (Nina was away at
the time, in Lausanne, where she'd just begun her training in
a hotel school.) So Clara put the money into three different
savings accounts at three different banks, and regarded it as
untouchable. Nina, on the other hand, gave all her inheritance—she was in love—to her Rüdiger, who borrowed the
rest of the finance, built the house and recorded it, for the sake
of simplicity, in his name in the land register. He demanded a
rent from Clara and my father that left Clara feeling dizzy—
but she couldn't resist Rüdiger either, and she loved Nina—
while my father who, down to the last rappen, earned exactly
the amount the apartment cost, couldn't have been in more
wholehearted agreement. Never in his life had he lived so
splendidly! Thrilled, he walked through the rooms flooded
with natural light, looking for the best place for his desk, while
Clara spent long hours at the bedroom window, looking across

at the forest, behind which the lake was concealed. 'Wonderful, isn't it?' my father would say, and Clara would nod. — A
Herr Jehle, the owner of *Wohnbedarf*, visited the house more
and more often; soon became more of a friend. The furniture
his firm sold was designed by Mies van der Rohde or by Le
Corbusier, and his catalogues looked like art books. No prices
were indicated. Soon, bookshelves were filling the walls perfectly, and the desk — a new one, with a black surface, and
drawers that rolled on wheels — found a place in a niche in the
living room. In its brightest corner — outside, beyond the glass,
were luscious green meadows or golden yellow crops, and in
the distance, the far distance, the town, and the river, lost in
the mist — a coffee table on chrome-steel supports that wob-
bled and swayed when my father so much as stirred his coffee. Around the table, tubular steel armchairs. A couch with
a throw, the patterns and colours of which looked Russian or
maybe Arabic. Cushions in all kinds of colours. Upright
lamps. Small varnished tables. A cupboard with a sliding door
made of blue glass; in it, plates, glasses, a siphon bottle. A rug
from Persia or Afghanistan, the latter *not* from Herr Jehle,
who would have nothing but parquet flooring or slabs of Por-
tuguese marble. At the door that led to the terrace and into
the garden stood a gramophone, a radio and gramophone in
one, Marconi's masterpiece, made of walnut, the size of a side-
board, and in use day and night. My father was the meloma-
niac, not Clara. (Clara, though, went to all the concerts of the
Young Orchestra.) Always; simply, always; Mozart, Beethoven,
Brahms could be heard throughout the house; or Lalo's *Sym-
phonie espagnole*, or *Firebird*. Records could be stacked on the
record player, they clattered, one after the other, down onto the
turntable. The arm moved across automatically; my father had-
n't even to get up from his desk. 'Great opera choruses'! Jussi

Björling! Leo Slezak! And records with Enrico Caruso that
were already old back then! Hits by Zarah Leander, Marlene
Dietrich, like 'Ich wollt' ich wär' ein Huhn', 'Ich bin die fesche
Lola' or 'Das ist die Liebe der Matrosen'. Jazz. My father par-
ticularly liked Benny Goodman and, above all, Teddy Wilson.
Phil Heymans, too, when he discovered her Elite Special
recordings. — By the time the apartment was furnished, Clara
had come a good bit closer to being as impoverished as she'd
reckoned she was. My father was enjoying this new-found
luxury to the full. The architect and Herr Jehle showed the
house to three or four journalists and photographers from
Werk and *Graphis*, then everyday life could begin. — My father
and Clara were with Nina and Rüdiger almost every day. Winter had arrived, meanwhile, and they messed around in the garden, throwing snowballs at one another. In the evenings, they
sat up in the first floor, drinking sherry or Martini. Nina
clapped with joy whenever Rüdiger, who wore bright suits and
could be incredibly charming, yet again praised Clara's beauty,
so making her blush. My father laughed, too. Rüdiger loved
women, and he loved dogs. Immediately after their wedding,
he'd surprised Nina with two mastiffs, Astor and Carino, who
smashed Chinese vases to pieces when they raced across the
slippery floor and went sliding into the bends. My father was
afraid of them; of Carino, above all, who would confront him,
baring his teeth, and growling. 'What's the matter?' Rüdiger
would say, patting the monster's snout. 'My Carino wouldn't
do anything to you.' (He'd the habit of saying 'my house' and
'my office' and 'my wife' too.) — Spring came, and Clara
headed into the garden. It was enormous and full of wild
blackberries, hazel bushes and nettles. She cleared it, section
by section, digging so many stones out that they formed a
mountain. The dry wood she burnt. My father never went into

the garden, not even when Clara called to him that the air was magnificent. He only ever breathed through a cigarette, in any case; and preferred to stay at his desk. He hammered the keys of his Continental typewriter, raising his head at the end of every sentence to see where his wife was. She was standing, in her gardener's apron, in the smoke from her fire, leaning on the handle of her spade. She was staring into the flames. Her lips moving, as if she were praying.

IN FEBRUARY 1936, on the Sunday before Carnival, the archi-tect, who'd been upstairs, dropped in on Clara and my father, making it quick. Or rather: Clara wasn't there — she'd gone to a concert — and my father was sitting at his typewriter, trans-lating *La Légende du Moine en rut* into German. The architect, really red in the face, stormed into the living room, shouting that Rüdiger had just paid him his fee, and it was exactly the amount they'd agreed upon years ago when no one could have known what a real slog the house would be. He'd bust a gut, but Rüdiger hadn't paid him a rappen more than agreed. The architect was gasping for breath. He thought that was shabby, exploitative and bourgeois. He wasn't a dog, after all — and the fascist mastiffs had probably cost more than his entire fee. My father nodded. He invited the architect to take a seat in one of the tubular steel armchairs, and opened a bottle of Cor-ton Clos du Roi, a fine, ready-for-drinking burgundy, one of thirty-six bottles he'd been talked into purchasing a few weeks ago by a salesman who'd fought his way out to this house that stood alone in the wilderness, and, despite his exhaustion, behaved like the king on the label. The crate full of bottles had arrived the day before, accompanied by a bill that was written by hand and looked like the Edict of Nantes. The

amount on the bill ate up about three times my father's
monthly salary. Clara had known nothing about the purchase;
and, with an unusually high voice, worked out for her husband
by when they'd both be down and out—that is, by 1 January
1945, if he continued the way he was going, and the prices of
basic foodstuffs remained stable; and extracted the promise
from him that he'd keep the Corton Clos du Roi for very, very
special occasions. This evening, my father reckoned, was such
an occasion. What was more: he needed to check whether the
salesman had cheated him when he'd praised the wine in the
highest terms. My father raised his glass—his nose was
already telling him that the wine was wonderful—sipped,
swallowed and gave a satisfied grunt, whereas the architect
knocked his back without noticing what a sumptuous wine he
was drinking. He was getting too worked up about Rüdiger,
more worked up still when my father said he was absolutely
right: he himself couldn't stand those brutes of animals either.
'Exploitation! A classic case of exploitation!' the architect
shouted. He was on his second glass before he calmed down a
little—my father, happy with his purchase, was sipping, still, at
his first—and began to leave Rüdiger alone. Now, for as long
as it took to drink all of the second glass, they discussed the
endeavours of the Soviet Union which, in keeping with its
five-year plans, was planting as many crops as were required
to prevent the Russian people from starving. (My father was
one glass behind the architect but now keeping up with him.)
The architect's third glass, and my father's second, focused on
Stalin, about whom the architect wouldn't have a bad word
spoken. He knew all the Resolutions of the Central Commit-
tee, and had adopted them for himself. My father said the
Soviet Union was the Soviet Union, and Switzerland was
Switzerland, he only had to think of the General Strike, the

dead, he'd still been a boy at the time, a big boy, but he'd heard the shots fired by the soldiers, soldiers who had been fetched—deliberately—from the furthest-flung parts of the country so that they'd have no inhibitions about firing at the striking workers. He'd run to the square outside the cathedral, he had, and seen the puddles of blood on the cobbles. By the time they'd reached their fourth and third glass, they'd moved on to the economic crisis and how the unemployed weren't getting any assistance whatsoever; by the time of their fifth and fourth glasses, to the struggle for the forty-eight-hour week— there were still employers, even now, who in all seriousness tried to defend a fifty-six-hour week; and while the architect sucked at his sixth glass, my father put in a bit of a spurt and pulled level with him. They talked about Mussolini and Hitler, repulsive creeps who were, equally, ridiculous and terrible. About the Popular Front in France. About Stakhanov who, when it came to mining coal, had fulfilled 1,300 per cent of the norm. About the public trials in Moscow, and the opportunity they gave the bourgeoisie to spread lies about Stalin. My father had now finally had his political awakening. In favour of Communism. When he opened the third bottle—he and his new comrade were discussing the brainless Social Democrats: how they were duped by any crawling by the Right, and had their tails between their legs at the slightest hint of any threat—Clara came home. She stared at the wine bottles and, without a word, disappeared to the bathroom. By the time the third bottle was empty too—the subject of conversation: how it had been impossible for the radical thinkers on the Left to develop a more offensive consciousness since the Communist Party had been elected to three town councils—it was three in the morning. In an hour, at four on the dot, Carnival began. They jumped onto bikes—the architect onto Clara's—

and rode down into town. In the dark; without lights; the architect behind the silhouette of my father, who knew, but couldn't see, the way. In the streets around the market square, tens of thousands of people, as always — it being sacrosanct — for Carnival, and the beginning of Lent. They were in coats and caps, it being icy cold. The noses, ears and fingers of the two new friends had been frozen off even as they cycled down, and so they went straight to the Ticino, to the Thieves' Den, which — given that outside, in the pitch dark, the traditional marches of the drummers and fifers were beginning, and no one wanted to miss this magic moment — was not yet completely overrun. They even got two seats at the architect's usual table where one of his friends jumped up from his seat when he saw them; a painter, with red eyes, who shouted heaven had sent them, for tomorrow — as the architect knew, of course — the big masked ball would be taking place in every room in the building, and the decorations were not only not ready yet but also actually hardly begun, and of the group of painters — that is, the Group 33, which was organizing the celebration, at its own expense — not a single one had turned up the previous evening when they'd planned to decorate everything beautifully — *picobello* — together. He wouldn't accept the excuse that they'd all been painting lanterns and laminating masks for weeks, and hadn't managed to finish those last night either. He'd handed over masks, the paint on which was still wet, to the Breo clique. (And, indeed, outside the windows of the Ticino, they could now see and hear a procession of drummers and fifers passing, with a gigantic lantern, carried by four porters and lit from within by a hundred and more candles, the style of which could easily be attributed to one member of the group. — Moreover, they all lived more or less all year round from the commissions they received for Carnival.) —

'Help,' the painter said, 'I need help, and I've reached the stage I'll accept any I get.' And so the architect and my father finished off their coffee — putting schnapps in the coffee, God knows why, was known as 'finishing it off' — and went up to the first floor with the painter and made themselves so useful — they'd the verve and full command of a situation that drunks often have — that the painter soon stopped giving them instructions. He was standing at a wall covered with brown wrapping paper, and painting an ideal landscape, a paradise full of lions, tigers, lakes, drummers and fifers that, apart from their instruments and incredible masks, were naked, for they were all Adams and Eves, striding off beneath the trees. These were palm trees, not firs, but painted, nonetheless, in the style of Kirchner, for the painter had spent two summers and a winter with the master in Davos. Kirchner had sworn at him the entire time, and told him, as he left, that his lack of talent knew no limits, and that he painted like an animal. (Despite that, a painting by this pupil of Kirchner was to appear with the name of his master at the exhibition of degenerate art in Munich, an honour at which neither Kirchner nor his pupil protested.) — Later, in the early afternoon — my father was on a ladder, pinning balloons and streamers to the ceiling — another painter turned up, a Surrealist, sporting a *béret basque*, who immediately tackled the other wall and at such a speed that he'd soon caught up with Kirchner's pupil. Giraffes with the heads of apes; apes with the faces of members of the Federal Council; members of the Federal Council lying with curvaceous dames who had fire blowing out of their mouths and behinds. — The architect, all the while, was still calculating the mass of a cubist sculpture he wanted to hang above the entrance; he was having problems with the golden rule and kept correcting his sketch. — Around Tuesday lunchtime, another painter appeared,

a woman this time. The room was already looking really wonderful, all the walls, and the ceiling, too, were painted in all the
colours of the spectrum, so she got to work on the stairway,
starting off by painting the banister a garish red. (The latter
still wasn't dry in the evening, and so many guests entered the
room with a red left hand.) This painter had just returned from
Paris, where she'd travelled with a friend and immediately
fallen into the claws of Man Ray. The same boy had started to
talk to the two women — no wonder, their hunger for the won-
ders of the city was spilling from their every pore — on their
second or third evening, in Deux Magots or Cafe Flore, a
bohemian haunt, in any case, that only the initiated knew, and
dragged them back to his atelier. There, he photographed both;
nude, of course; and the painter, oddly, who was barely twenty,
and pretty as a picture, was a poorer model than her friend,
though the latter was more the bony type, and from Berne.
The pictures with her, herself, were, nevertheless, to become
iconic photographs. (Her friend, by the way, also became famous. She was the one with the cup, covered in fur.) My father
then helped this painter who, without hesitation, let him have
paints and brushes. They spoke French to one another: my
father, because he'd already been awake for twenty-eight
hours and still wasn't sober; the painter, because she was
imbued with life in Paris. (She punned, however, only in her
dialect. She was a master at it, and as my father too didn't miss
a chance to play with words — not stopping at the most awful
examples, either — puns were going backwards and forwards
between them, constantly; and, in the end, they spoke more
German than French.) — When, at nine in the evening, the
first masks turned up, the decoration was finished. It was
a masterpiece that took in the room on the first floor, an
adjoining room, the stairway and the restaurant itself, where

they'd worked while bar service had continued. The customers hadn't been put off by an artist clambering about in front of them, on their tables; and hanging paper monsters and masks with grotesque faces from the ceiling. — The architect was still standing, pensively, in front of the statue that he'd already mounted, and then dismounted, several times. — It was too late for my father to head home again, and Clara — who'd cleared away the Corton-Clos-du-Roi bottles and washed the glasses — was dying a thousand deaths, not only because she knew — this knowledge was carved deeply into every native of the town, like a law of biblical power — that, at Carnival time, everything and anything was possible — drunken capers, obscene language in public, adultery — and that you just had to accept it, whether delighted by it or gnashing your teeth. That my father could be at the artists' party in the Thieves' Den didn't occur to her, and she spent the evening, looking out the window at the protective forest. Her husband, meanwhile, was raging his way through one room after another, drunk and floating and chatting. He danced with really beautiful women who were dressed up as old aunts or water sprites, and several times, too, with the lady painter. He then fell asleep, dancing a quickstep, on his partner's shoulder; and when he woke again, in a corner of the kitchen, the sun was shining brightly beyond the windows. Waitresses were climbing over him, and Luigi, the landlord, was juggling eight pans on his three-flame stove. My father was wearing a clown's costume, though he'd no idea how he'd got into it; and he had a headache. He gave himself a shake, and had to walk home; there wasn't a tram fare in the pocket of his costume, and he'd forgotten both their bikes were outside the Ticino. Clara was still — or, again — at the window, but gave him a friendly welcome; it was Carnival, after all. The clown was his explanation for everything. He threw himself on his bed, and was soon fast asleep again. — On the Thursday evening, at the end of all the carnivalling, the architect and Kirchner's pupil brought back the bikes. Beaming happily, they told them how great the party my father could remember only vaguely had been. All the rooms full to bursting, fantastic music — the Saloon Stompers, featuring the incomparable Heini Müller on trumpet, who worked for an insurance company for the rest of the year — and, in the early morning, the last individual masks had played football out on the street with the very balloons my father had pinned to the wall. Two dozen Pierrots and hobgoblins and wild men, but not a single clown, had passed the balloons to one another, the balloons floating gracefully from foot to foot. Here and there, one had burst — especially because of the wild men's clogs — and, once the last of the balloons had also ended up in tatters, they'd finally gone home. — The architect, Kirchner's pupil, the Surrealist and the lady painter now often visited Clara and my father. They were all passionate artists, open to anything new, and ardent supporters of Socialist goals. Communists: some of them, more so; others, less so. This year's Carnival had made a communist of my father, too. True, Kirchner's pupil, whose ideological views were more radical than those of the architect, called him, first, a bourgeois intellectual, and then, once, even a drawing-room communist, but, like all the others, he felt at ease up in that bright apartment at the edge of town. When spring came, and with it a warm sun, he put up his canvas in the garden and painted Clara and my father drinking coffee: Clara, lying in a yellow dress on a deck chair; and my father, sitting at the red garden table, reading a book. On the table, as in real life, stood the coffee machine that looked like a test tube from a chemistry lab. In the background, a dog was running in very green grass, a splodge of black paint. (In the real world, its name was Hobby, and it was, in every respect, the exact opposite of Rüdiger's mastiffs, one of which, that is, Astor, in the picture, was lying beside Clara and staring past the viewer with a similarly vacant look.) Right at the back, the forest that protected them from avalanches. The sky, a bold brush-stroke. — He was in a kind of ecstasy, the painter, because — with this painting — he'd moved on, left Kirchner behind. He painted it in *one* afternoon, stayed for supper and then announced that he wanted to call it *L'après-midi bourgeois*. Clara was beaming, my father looked skeptical. But both were agreed that today was a very special occasion and uncorked a bottle of Corton Clos du Roi. — At the height of summer, Kirchner's pupil painted the picture again, a second version, in his newly acquired colouring, for which he took more time. Again, my father was reading a book; again, Clara was staring into a void; again, Astor was beside her. It was just that, in the background, Hobby, the little dog, had vanished. The second picture appealed less to Clara and my father. — All the painters, including the lady one, were so pleased with my father that they asked him to be the group's secretary, or agent, or jack-of-all-trades. My father said yes, without a moment's hesitation. There had been no mention of any payment; and he expected and received none. The painters laughed and clapped his shoulders; the lady painter gave him a kiss. — That same summer, there was a shish-kebab night in the garden (on the first hot weekend; not long before, Hitler's troops had marched into the Rhineland), that all the members of the group attended, including the two painters Clara and my father didn't know yet, a robust Constructivist, working at the time exclusively with wire — shaky creations in all kinds of sizes, covered in plaster sometimes — and a very young man, who suffered from tuberculosis, had withdrawn to the Weinland region and was regarded as the genius of the group. Their wives and girlfriends came, too. But also guests from Clara's more sheltered days, a plump man in a Colonial-style suit, for example, who was called Wern, and whom Clara knew from the time she'd been the right hand of the conductor of the Young Orchestra, that ensemble in which everything was new: the music, the musicians and the conductor, Edwin Schimmel. Wern was close to the latter, whereas Clara, since handing in her notice, had had no further contact with the orchestra and its boss. No, she did, she'd been made an honorary member—to reward her for all her unpaid work—and still went to all the concerts.—There were also four friends from her schooldays, and their husbands who were doctors or lawyers.—A fire was burning in the long hollows, the wine was flowing and the men carved skewers from hazel branches, on which the pieces of meat were roasted. The two mastiffs and Hobby were trotting around somewhere. Yes, Rüdiger and Nina were there, too. Nina was welcomed immediately by the painters; and Rüdiger discovered an acquaintance or two among the husbands of Clara's schoolfriends. Everyone was sitting, or lying, on woollen blankets. At first, they talked about the Frontist movement, who had smashed the shop window of Samuel Grün Erben, the best shop for shirts in the town, but they soon forgot the current misery. Much laughter. A full moon in the sky, their faces all flickering red in the light of the fires. Things being called from group to group. Every so often, one of the schoolfriends screeched with laughter, at a joke, or because one of the painters had stolen a kiss. The women ate with their hands, the men drank from the bottles: not the Corton Clos du Roi but a table wine that Clara's uncle produced in Piedmont, and that tasted good. Happy, my father was fooling around and, at one point, spoke in rhyme for such a long time that the lady painter warned him 'One more rhyme, and it's home-time!' and my father switched to prose. Clara, serious, kept an eye on whether their guests had everything they needed, and was the only person still to be drinking her first glass of wine at the end of the night. The party continued all night, and, when the guests set out on their way home, the sun was rising from behind the forest. Clara and my father stood, arm in arm, and watched as their friends, chattering, and gently swaying, disappeared over the nearby horizon, at the point where the road began to descend towards the town. For a while they could still hear their polyphonic singing; first, 'Our life is like the journey of the wanderer through the night'; and later, distant now already, 'Santa Lucia'. They went to bed and made love drunkenly, hungrily, as if for the first time. When my father woke up, around noon, and blinked out the window: lying on the blankets, up close to one another, and in a deep sleep, were the Surrealist and the lady painter. The Surrealist was on his back and had his mouth wide open, whereas the lady painter had curled up so tightly, her now loose, strawberry blonde hair was covering her entire body. — My father made coffee and drank it at that red garden table. He watched the two sleeping. There was still smoke from the fires in the hollows. By the time he'd drunk his second cup and lit his third cigarette the Surrealist woke up, blinked into the sunlight and recognized my father. He beamed, lifted himself up off the ground and bumped into the lady painter, who also opened her eyes, sat up and began to laugh. 'Good morning,' my father said, though it was already well into the afternoon. When all three had emptied their bowls, and the Surrealist and the lady painter had also had their first cigarette of the day, Clara turned up with gummed-up eyes. She was wearing a dressing gown and was barefoot.

She sat down at the table, at which—hard to say, why—the conversation now dried up. They all had a hangover. The Surrealist and the painter got their bits and pieces together, and my father and Clara accompanied them to the gate. They joked a little as they said goodbye, and then the two headed off, in the middle of the road: the Surrealist, in his badly creased trousers and his *béret basque*; and the painter, barefoot, her shoes in her hand. Her loose hair reached down over her behind. When their heads vanished over the horizon, Hobby, who had been waiting between my father and Clara, ran off after the two others, stopping where the road vanished into nowhere. A black silhouette that used a paw, first, to wave goodbye; then to scratch behind its ears.—That evening, my father, as he, actually, always did, went to bed early, and Clara, as usual, went much later. She loved the quiet hours of the beginning of the night. He didn't ever notice her creeping into bed, and didn't that night either. Unlike any other night, he woke at two or three in the morning. Clara wasn't in bed, and she wasn't in the bathroom or the living room either. He went out onto the terrace and saw her in the light of the still almost-full moon, coming up the garden, in a dress that was sticking to her legs because it was wet up to her thighs. 'I couldn't sleep,' she said. 'I went for a walk.' My father grunted. White-faced, she walked past him and he returned to bed. He'd been asleep again for a long time when she lay down beside him. When, three or four hours later, he was disturbed by a hammering headache and got up, she was lying there, with her eyes closed and breathing gently. He crept on tiptoe to the door, and she turned in the bed and, in a deep sleep, sighed. He smiled, despite his migraine, and went to the bathroom to take a tablet.

NOT LONG AFTER THAT, my father succeeded in setting up an exhibition for the group. It was the first time, for all the members, that their work was to be shown in public. The Bittner & Hill Gallery was very respected and run by the widow of one of the founders—either Kurt Bittner, or Frédéric Hill—who had reverted, however, to using her maiden name. Rudescu. On a single afternoon, my father dragged Madame Rudescu around the studios of Kirchner's pupil, the Surrealist, the Constructivist wire sculptor, the lady painter, even the consumptive painter, though the latter lived far out in the Weinland region. With a dark face, Madame Rudescu trudged around the studios, turned pictures round, raised them close to her eyes and groaned. She left, each time, without saying goodbye. On the way back from the final studio, that of the artist with consumption, she looked so furious that my father finally gave up all hope. When they arrived at the gallery, though, and my father made to say goodbye, she muttered, not any more happily, that she'd do the exhibition, and pushed a contract across to my father, the terms of which couldn't have been any more beneficial for her. '*I* am taking all the risk,' she said when my father pointed shyly at the percentage she'd retain in the event of a sale. '*I*'ll set the prices.' She did then set them, and so high that all the painters, and my father, too, were convinced they would manage to sell nothing.—When, a month later, my father was hanging the pictures with Madame Rudescu—the painters intended coming later, of course, to re-hang them all—a car stopped, like an apparition, outside the door: a Maybach with whitewall tyres. My father stared, with one of the lady painter's pictures in his hand, out the shop window. A chauffeur rushed round the outside of the car, tore his cap from his head and opened the door, and out climbed a lady in a fur and a big hat. Removing her gloves, she entered the

gallery, greeting Madame Rudescu very warmly, and it turned
out she was Tildi Schimmel, the wife of the conductor of the
Young Orchestra, and the heir to the firm she'd brought into
the marriage with Schimmel. She was the most important collector in the town, the richest as well as the most competent,
and wanted a look at the paintings before the opening, a right
she, but of course, had the nerve to demand, and that, but of
course, was granted. She wandered round the gallery with my
father, chatting about anything and everything, looked at this
and that picture—for the most part, the pictures were still
stood against the wall—scrutinized a large-format painting by
the Surrealist and said, yes, she'd just been to Paris, and Pablo
had had a terrible quarrel with Marie-Thérèse, because of
Dora, but then all three had gone to visit Alberto, after all, in
pouring rain. Basically, Pablo was a draughtsman who also
painted; and Alberto, a sculptor who painted. Only Henri,
whom she perhaps really did rate most, was a painter who
painted, and therefore very close to his true being; and what
was more: he didn't ask for outrageous prices like Pablo. My
father, who, after a while, had realized whom she meant, nodded and said he loved the South, every painter who had to do
with the South; but you couldn't get him to like Munch or
Nolde if you paid him. The wife of the conductor, who was also
the director of the firm, laughed. 'I like your opinions,' she said.
'Come to supper. Thursday. Just a few people. Bring your wife
with you.—You come, too, Elena.' She turned to the owner of
the gallery, who blushed. On the way out, she pointed to a few
pictures—'That one, that one and that one up the back'—two
large formats by the Surrealist, and a darkly eccentric landscape by the painter from the Weinland region, which were,
indeed, the best three pictures in the exhibition. She pulled on
her gloves and climbed into her car. The chauffeur closed the

door, put his cap on, went round the outside of the car—this time choosing the route via the rear—climbed in, and the Maybach drove off without a sound. The beautiful profile of Frau Schimmel at the rear window.—On Thursday, a few days later, Clara and my father took up the invitation. They'd to take a taxi, there was no other way of reaching the estate, situated in a park full of very old trees, outside the town, and high above the lake. Torches burning in the garden; high, lit windows; when the taxi stopped at the portal. They walked across the gravel and were received by a butler who took their coats. They were standing in a brightly lit hall, and flying down the staircase came the lady of the house in a scarlet dress. She beamed at them both—'Oh, Clara! I can just say Clara to you, can't I? Edwin has told me so much about you!'—and invited them into the drawing room. Bright light, again, slippery parquet flooring. Pictures on all the walls by Matisse and Klee and Kandinsky and Miró. A large still life by Cézanne. My father and Clara were still admiring the pictures when the other guests, as if it had been pre-arranged, all arrived at the same time: Elena Rudescu, wearing a revealing dress made of a shimmering greeny-purple silk; the Surrealist, who was still in his working clothes but had cleaned his shoes; and a not-exactly-young-any-more, tall gentleman in a dark suit, whose name my father didn't catch, and who, if he properly understood the conversations that followed, had something to do with a bank in Geneva and, like the lady of the house, was a passionate art collector. His hobby seemed to be the Italian *Cinquecento*; at any rate, even if people were discussing Mondrian or Vallotton, he kept coming back to Michelangelo and Signorelli. He had arrived with a very young woman whom my father regarded, at first, as his lover, then as his daughter, but who was, in fact, his wife. They were all standing with a glass in their hand. They were all smiling as they talked about the weather, now, in autumn, being chillier already. About it being a pity that with there being a new moon that very evening, they wouldn't be able to enjoy the no doubt magnificent view down onto the lake. — Tildi Schimmel was just asking the Surrealist whether he'd seen the Impressionists' exhibition in the Orangerie — the Surrealist said no — when their host entered the drawing room. Edwin Schimmel. He swept up to his guests as if they were his prey. Smiling through closed lips, like a pencil stroke. Perfectly combed black hair. Looking at the world through bright blue eyes. He kissed his wife's hand, greeted Madame Rudescu with a slight bow and turned on his heel to Clara. 'Clara!' he exclaimed. 'Long time no see! How are you then?'

'I'm pregnant,' Clara said.

'How nice,' Edwin Schimmel said. 'You always wanted a child.' He turned to my father. 'And you, Sir, are the proud father?'

'I hope so,' said my father. 'I'm hearing about it for the first time.'

The first course was *Bisque de homard*. My father declined and watched the others spoon it up. The second course consisted of porcini and roasted hot peppers, which my father also declined. When he said no to the main course, too, a *filet de veau en croûte*, Tildi Schimmel asked him what he did eat. 'A piece of Emmental and some bread is what I'd like most,' he said. Tildi Schimmel looked at the butler, who raised his eyebrows, disappeared from the dining room and returned a few moments later with a piece of Emmental on a plate. Bread was already on the table. He put the plate in front of my father, who said 'Thank you,' and began to eat. — Tildi Schimmel got

each and every one present caught up in a kind of interrogation, a warm-hearted questioning about whatever was important to them, currently. So she spoke to my father about the
upcoming exhibition, and told the Surrealist he was the only
talented one in the group. It was her style, simply, to say
things as they were. He'd got something, really; the others,
however . . . She held out both hands. The Surrealist laughed
and asked why she'd bought a painting by the young genius
then, the one with TB. 'That's why,' she said. He was sure to
die young, and she'd then own of his very few paintings; and
it wasn't as if he was that bad. — The banker from Geneva was
speaking meanwhile to Madame Rudescu, one of whose
clients he, clearly, also was, about the pictures being hung too
close together in the Louvre and the Uffizi. Yes, Madame
Rudescu said. Hanging them properly was half the battle; and
yet hardly anyone had the knack of it, least of all the artist
himself. — Clara smiled when Tildi Schimmel asked her if she
missed working with the orchestra. 'No, no,' she said. There
was a time for everything. — The banker's wife ate without a
word, bite by bite, just raising her eyes, sometimes, very
briefly, to look at her husband. — Edwin Schimmel hardly said
a word, either. It looked like, in his thoughts, he was already
onto the next day, a meeting of the administrative board or an
orchestra rehearsal. He did, indeed, answer when the banker's
wife asked him, at one point: did he, too, have as much work
to do as her husband? Yes, he did, he guessed so; tomorrow,
at any rate, at the crack of dawn, he was travelling to London
to conduct the 'Messias', *The Messiah*. In London, of all places!
And at the Albert Hall! With the London Symphony and the
King's Men Chorus. Now, everyone was looking, including
Clara, who had turned red. My father told the anecdote of the
first-ever performance, when the King, some George or the

other, or an Edward, had been so moved that he'd stood up when he heard the beginning of the Hallelujah. And, ever since, audiences in Britain have always stood for Handel's Hallelujah. Always, and all over the country. 'If they don't do it for you,' my father said to Edwin Schimmel, 'no one can blame *you*. You'll be standing, in any case.' Everyone stopped eating and looked at Edwin. My mother nudged my father with her foot under the table. 'Why do you keep kicking me?' he said. The pencil stroke that was Edwin's mouth suddenly broadened so much that his lips parted and his teeth became visible. He was laughing. Everyone laughed, most of all Tildi Schimmel who had tears running down her face. Only my father remained serious. — On the way home, in the taxi, Clara began to cry, insisting he'd shown her up, Karl, what on earth had made him do that? Emmental, at a meal like that! What would Edwin's wife be thinking of her now; not to mention Edwin. — 'How come you told him you're pregnant?' my father said. '*Are* you pregnant?'

'Yes,' Clara said.

'And why did you tell *him* that?'

'I don't know.'

'You don't know?'

'No.'

THEN THE CHILD WAS BORN, me, and my father was pleased. Pleased beyond measure, so much so that he never called me by the name with which I was baptized but always invented new pet names for me. The names of animals, but not only. He used so many different names, in fact, that I responded to everything. Be it Bear or Dwarf. It also went without saying for him, though — nothing else had ever entered his head — that all the care and attention the child needed was the woman's job. Clara's job. The breast-feeding, the bathing, the rocking, the caring for. He, after all, had his work. He was now a teacher at a newly opened grammar school that passed up teaching Greek altogether; didn't promote Latin as strongly as other, equivalent schools focusing on the classics did; and set greatest store by those languages that the curriculum called 'living'. He was teaching French; now and then, also German. (Right at the beginning, the headteacher wanted to palm off two hours per week of both Religion and Gym on him, too. But my father, an atheist with a childhood that had made him well versed in the Bible, answered every argument the Principal had with a Bible quotation until he gave up and released him from Religion. Which left Gym. He held two or three lessons, but after giving the first swimming lessons dressed in a coat and hat — he couldn't swim — he was relieved of Gym also.) — His university career had come to nothing. The old professor, Herr Tappolet, wasn't even thinking of dying, and when finally, way past the usual age, he was given emeritus status, my father and he had fallen out so completely and utterly that he made a point of recommending a very dry outside lecturer from Tübingen as his successor. A *Song of Roland* specialist. The same boy was then also selected, and my father told Herr Tappolet what he thought of that selection, that is, nothing. Herr Tappolet's successor, as was well known, knew about nothing but his Olifant, zilch, and he, Herr Tappolet, was doing exactly what all the other big-name professors did, that is, supporting the most stupid successor in order to shine on, themselves, for as long as possible in the memory of the generations that followed. Now he'd got going, my father also informed his boss as to what he thought of his book about Tristan, that is, also nothing. His hypothesis—that the original version of *Tristan et Yseult* was a collective creation and the work of the French people—wasn't tenable, and his attempt, in the appendix, to translate the ancient epic into modern French, had failed miserably. When Herr Tappolet muttered well okay, perhaps, he'd yet, though, to see a single line of my father's post-doctoral thesis, the latter roared, 'And nor will you! You'll be the last person to!' and stormed out of the Department, slamming the door with such force that the medieval plaster rained from the ceiling. Looking neither left nor right, he trudged home on his bike, put all his materials—a few metres of excerpts, transcriptions and interpretations—in a chest he then locked with a springlock, the key of which he threw out the window. The nuns and monks were over and done with, for the rest of his life.—He applied to ten schools—he had, after all, a teaching qualification—but without success, and began to prepare himself for living, in the near and also distant future, off inherited money when he was selected for a post, after all, at a grammar school specializing in modern languages. He proved to be a passionate teacher. He was bathed in sweat after every lesson and, himself, excited by the material he'd used. (That said, he didn't bother about the curricula especially, and preferred speaking German, to French.)—He was still out and about on behalf of the group, of course. And now he'd got rid of the monks, nuns and Tappolet, he threw himself with renewed energy into the task of translating those books he especially loved, and of which there was either not a German version or not a decent one. He began with the diaries of André Gide that had just come out, and which thrilled him, and learnt only once he was finished that the likes of copyright existed, that he should have obtained the translation rights and that he'd never have got them. Someone else had been commissioned ages ago, and had almost completed his translation. (My father, when it was published, found it atrocious.) So he put his manuscript on top of the chest —since, of course, he couldn't open it—and threw himself into the classics that anyone who wanted to could translate; into forgotten and hardly known writers, above all; and, first of all, into *Ulenspiegel* by Charles De Coster, about whom he was passionate. He worked in the morning before going to school—though it began at seven-fifteen in summer; and in winter, all the same, at eight—and on his free afternoons, and on Sundays, and was able to translate in his head. He knew the words of the original always some ten or twenty lines in advance, and could also easily remember his German version. When he arrived home, he would drop his briefcase, without a word to anyone, and head, as if under hypnosis, to the corner where he worked. Only once he'd typed up what he'd piled up in his head, in a standing position, and with one finger, did he take his hat off and greet Clara and the child. 'Hello, Marmot!' I was lying in a cradle that, in fact, was always in the garden—it was summer now—watched by Astor, his chaps right above my face. Yes, I actually saw Astor more than anyone else.—Clara was a loving mother who kept strictly to the orders of the doctor, a Dr Massini, who repeated everything twice, 'Good day, good day,' he said when he arrived, and 'Two decilitres every two hours, two decilitres every two hours.' He was an expert in modern nutrition, and Clara fed her child every two hours and not a minute sooner. Even if it was screaming and screaming. That said, she couldn't wake up early. She simply couldn't. And so my father lifted me out of the cradle in the mornings, with his cigarette in his mouth, and, still mentally translating his text, gave me my bottle. Soon, Nina was doing that—who was a woman and didn't have a school to go to. Clara would come later, at about ten, and take the child in her arms. And hug and kiss it. — My father began, meanwhile, on the translation of the letters of Mariana Alcoforado, who had lived in the eighteenth or perhaps seventeenth century in a convent in Portugal — my father knew about nuns, after all — and whose passion for her lover knew no limits. She loved, loved like no other woman, and my father translated her invocations such that he almost caught fire himself.

ON 1 SEPTEMBER 1939, my father and Clara heard Hitler's voice coming from their Marconi radio. Hitler was barking that the Poles had attacked him; and that he'd been shooting back since 6 a.m. The war had begun. My father, soon to be thirty-seven and, to date, unfit for service, reported for duty at a training camp, in Aarau, together with a few other oldish men with weak hearts and a horde of twenty-year-olds so full of strength that they could lift their knapsacks with one hand. He learnt how to get up early (he could do that already), how to salute his superiors properly and how to get his carbine onto his shoulder in four movements. The movements had to sound like rifle shots, like quick cracks of a whip. When the whole company greeted their commanding officer with a rifle position, it sounded like *one* man. Like one man and my father, for his movements, as a rule, more than 100 per cent of the time, slotted home after the others'; and every now and then, he'd also drop his rifle. He then had to step forward, before the colonel, and demonstrate his grips. One, two, three, four. Of course, it all turned out so hopelessly un-warlike that he was soon ordered back to his rank; and to spend the evening in the kitchen. Washing dishes and peeling potatoes. The cook was a postman from Adelhofen, who didn't know why the roundup commission had made him the cook and yet who was trying to impress a recruit, a frail, pale-faced lad who, in civilian life, was a sauce specialist in the Hôtel des Trois Rois but who never spoke about food. No wonder there were no sauces either; the poor postman from Adelboden had zero-point-eight-five francs per soldier per day to play with, and had never learnt anything other than how to throw potatoes and carrots into boiling water. His eyes pleaded nevertheless when he looked through his hatch into the canteen. — My father was then delighted when, after a few weeks, already, he was declared to be suitably trained for emergency services and posted to the so-called Kessiloch, a forlorn place in the rocks, where, in the First World War, the soldiers had been so bored that every reachable piece of rock was more richly decorated than the Lascaux Grotto. No fleeing stags and mammoths, it's true; rather, artistically decorated coats of arms of Emmen and Boncourt, and the wide open legs of women. — My father had to stand, all alone, at the exit of a railway tunnel, the tracks of which led out onto a bridge that was mined. My father was responsible for ensuring that no enemy crawled through the tunnel; or climbed up out of the ravine, in which, far below, a torrent roared. He stood there in his *kaput* — a coat that weighed tons, and yet he froze — wearing his steel helmet and holding his carbine, loaded with live ammunition, on the narrow strip of gravel between the platform and the abyss. His feet were blocks of ice. Every now and then, he'd shout, 'Who goes there?' into the night, when an animal rustled past; and he'd hear only his heartbeat, in reply. When a train was coming, the tracks would begin to sing, then he'd hear a distant rumble, then a wind would blow from the tunnel, and, when it had become a storm, the train would thunder — like madness, itself — from the tunnel. Lights flashing past. The bridge would tremble, the bushes bend in the wind, even the fir hanging at an angle over the ravine would shiver, the trunk of which my father used to hold on tight. Had my father screamed, no one would have heard him. Once or twice, he did scream. — When spring came and the nights got warmer and he still hadn't had any leave and, after a night that lasted a particular eternity, he was relieved by an especially grumpy comrade, he suddenly decided, instead of going to bed, to get on the quartermaster's bike — regardless of whether or not the same one needed it — and he cycled like a madman through ravines, forests and meadows until he got home, where Clara was standing, in a white dress, in the garden, in a sea of flowers, picking daffodils, tulips and anemones. A huge bouquet in one arm. Their child, me, was standing, clinging to one of her legs, and staring, like her, at his father as if he were a ghost. The latter threw his bike into the bushes and came running over the meadow — crushing daisies and corn poppies — took Clara by an arm, and dragged her into the house after him. They were both laughing or groaning and, as they ran, throwing away one item of clothing after another. The ammunition belt, the sandals, the uniform jacket, the white dress, the hobnailed boots. The child managed to cling to one of Clara's legs. Not until the corridor did it lose its grip, and end up between the field-grey trousers and a bundle, the size of a fist, that was a white silk undergarment. My father put the steel helmet on my head. I sat there in the dark, not knowing whether I felt great or overwhelmed. I could hear my brain roaring. I sang, my voice echoing beneath the dome of the helmet. I hit out. When I'd worked my way out into the light again, the bedroom door opened and my father and Clara came out; Clara looking out from under one of the arms of my father, who was wearing a military shirt, open at the front, and grey underpants. Clara's hair was down—it flowed down to her hips—she was wearing a salmon-coloured underskirt. My father laughed, lifted me—'There he is, now! The tiger!'—and kissed me, his cigarette still in his mouth. He put on his steel helmet, got into his trousers, shuffled with his legs apart, and closing all his buttons, over to his shoes, tied his laces and followed the trail of clothes back to the garden. Overall, belt, bayonet, ammunition pouch. From a good distance, among the flowers, he was a fully fledged soldier again, if one who had done his buttons up the wrong way. Clara had her dress on again, too.—At the garden gate, the other women, who lived in the house, had gathered. Which is to say, only women lived in the house. Rüdiger had been called up too, he was a member of a military court and, every now and then, sent Nina short messages— that he needed clean hankies or his sunglasses—the sender's address always given as 'in the field'. He was somewhere in the Réduit, or in Lucerne, pondering over death sentences.— Nina, of course, was there, and I ran over to her. Beside her, like a guard of honour, Jo, Hildegard and Rösli, each of whom threw her arms round my father as he rushed to the bike. It was as if the scent of a man had lured them out of their caves. Rösli, the last to arrive, even licked my father—he was jumping onto his bike already—all over his face. He, though, wasn't for being delayed, and, pedalling with all his might, his head right down on the handlebars, set off down the roadway that led to the forest. He had, after all, to cover 100 kilometres again, through the meadows, forests, ravines, and be back at the Kessiloch in time for roll call. Nina, Hildegard, Jo and Rösli waved their hankies, hopping with excitement, as if *they* were the brides.—Clara stood there, all serious.—Jo was a beauty from Suriname, or some other Dutch colony, and the elder sister of Phil Heymans, who, although only about twenty, was already performing at the best jazz venues in Amsterdam. Both sisters had fled from the impending German invasion; and arrived barely a week ago. A comrade had insisted on them memorizing the address of Kirchner's pupil, strictly forbidding them from writing it down. That was why they were wandering around at dusk in Heuberg—Jo thought it was number 36, whereas Phil was sure the house number began with a two—and then finally at the door of the studio: two wretched, beautiful women, with wet hair and raincoats and the one suitcase containing a little underwear and Phil's music. Kirchner's pupil put them up, and a few days later brought Jo to my father who, however, wasn't—not yet—there. Nina, fetched to help by a helpless Clara, immediately agreed to housing Jo in one of the attic rooms. She was glad Rüdiger was in the field, and suppressed the thought of having to tell him that Jo couldn't pay any rent, and that her papers weren't in order. Jo burst into tears and flung her arms round Nina's neck. (Phil, who continued to live at the home of Kirchner's pupil, and whose papers weren't in any better order, was soon singing—initially, at the weekends, then every evening—at the Singer, a dance hall on the market square, with Teddy Stauffer's quartet; he talked the director into hiring her as he urgently needed a female singer. What's more, Buddy Bertinat, on piano, had once accompanied her in Amsterdam and had very positive memories of her. 'Mickey's Round' and 'Without You, I'm Lonely' were her best numbers, and Stauffer immediately made both part of his repertoire.—The director agreed to Phil being hired on condition he'd no additional costs. There was a free meal in it for her, but nothing more.—From her first appearance, Phil was the star of the venue, and, after just a few days, was relieved of the requirement also to appear as part of the striptease numbers, the actual attraction of the establishment. She sang in a dress she borrowed from Nina and, two weeks later, was receiving an actual fee from the director that she shared — even if it was miserably little — with Jo, as her big sister had turned down the director's offer of stripping in place of Phil and, instead, lay every evening on Nina's couch, sleeping or sobbing.) — In the other attic apartment lived Hildegard, who, at school, had sat beside Clara and been her bosom friend — the two of them always thought, did, were, the same thing — and had become her successor with Edwin Schimmel, she, albeit, not in an honorary capacity but as a proper full-time secretary with a proper contract and a good salary. She'd probably fallen in love a little with this Edwin fellow. My father teased her about it, at times. The two girlfriends hardly ever spoke about him, however, certainly not about Hildegard's slight infatuation; at most, about certain things to do with work that Clara knew inside out: that the heating in the rehearsal room made noises if the caretaker turned it up too high, too quickly; or not to speak to Edwin in the hours leading up to the concert; things like that. — Rösli was Rüdiger and Nina's maid. She would not normally have kissed the same men as the other women of the house; but in the heat of the moment nobody noticed, neither Clara, nor Nina, nor Jo, nor Hildegard; not Rösli either; and not even my father.

MY FATHER GOT BACK TO THE KESSILOCH two minutes before roll call, all sweaty and out of breath. He was still in the saddle and panting for breath when, of all people, the quartermaster came storming out of the Command barracks, grabbed the handlebars of the bike without realizing it was his own and asked: did he, my father, know already? 'Have you heard

yet?' My father shook his head, got off the bike, thinking he'd
get three days' strict detention or be handed over to Rüdiger's
court, charged with purloining materials vital to the war
effort. But the quartermaster just threw the bike against the
barrack wall and wheezed: the *Wehrmacht* was about to invade
Switzerland. Tomorrow, or the day after. After Whitsun, at
the latest. The decision had been taken in Berlin, once and for
all; Hitler only had to give the signal. He knew this, the quartermaster, from a most reliable source, straight from the capital, Berne, from his brother who knew someone who was the
cousin of a confidant of a general. Or a colonel or a divisional
commander; a big shot, at any rate. He'd confided the information to him that very morning, the highest possible security
classification. My father wiped his forehead with his army
handkerchief, and nodded. It seemed logical, after all: Holland
and Belgium had been overrun in a few days, and now it was
France's turn. Why should the *Wehrmacht* attack Paris only
from the North and not also from the western border of
Switzerland? The liaison officer could go on as much as he
liked about no troop movements being discernible even far into
the Black Forest—an official bulletin from the intelligence
service, barely two hours old— but in no time the rumour
turned into the general certainty that the attack was imminent. — The roll call, normally a dull ritual before their free time
in the evening, now chilled their hearts. The colonel stood
before the troops, his face apoplectic—he, too, a victim of the
rumours—shouting that he knew that, should the foe attack
their beloved homeland, each and every one of them, like their
forefathers, would fight until the last drop of blood was spilt.
If it was God's will, Kessiloch would be the new Battle of Mor-
garten. They all saluted the flag, and my father, whose heart
was still racing, did his rifle drill so absentmindedly that he

did it perfectly. For the first time ever, the troop had sounded like one man. Like a single crack of a whip. Not that the colonel, or the comrades, or my father himself, noticed. They were all too troubled by the same thought: they all knew they wouldn't be able to defend their Kessiloch for even two hours. All it would take was three tanks and a flame-thrower troop, and they'd all be dead. All of those who, right now — 'Dismiss!' — were shuffling their way to the canteen, would be burnt to a cinder and be lying in the mud, and the tanks, as they withdrew, would crush their legs or their heads, without malicious intent. The colonel would be hanging from a tree, his head at an angle, his face redder than ever. — Things, no doubt, weren't any different in the rest of the country. How, for heaven's sake, were a few soldiers in their five bunkers at the border near Lörrach supposed to protect the town of Basel? What kind of heroic resistance would be required to prevent the German troops from passing St Gallen, Zurich and Berne on their way to the edge of the Alps? Were the old carbines going to achieve that? The bayonets, or the handful of cement cubes they called anti-tank obstacles? And what could the general, the general-staff guys and the Federal Councillors do, other than look out of the slits of the Réduit at the clouds of smoke, in the distance, from the burning towns where their soldiers and their wives and their children were living, or now no longer alive? — My father wanted to warn Clara. But how? Risk a second bicycle trip, now at night? — But Clara had heard the news even before my father; in fact, even as she was watching him cycle towards the forest. What had happened was: the milkman turned up, tooting his horn loudly, and at least an hour late, as he came over the horizon in his Citroën, shouting out the open window, and long before he stopped, that the Germans had arrived. They could turn up at any moment, ten thousand silhouettes beyond the cornfield. Schaffhausen was an inferno, children's corpses were floating in the Rhine. He got out—leaving the engine   running—and roared, not any more quietly, though right in front of the women now, that a most reliable source had told him so. It was impossible to doubt it. The Rhine Falls were red with the blood of the victims. His brother-in-law, seemingly, worked where military vehicles were serviced in Bern-Wabern, and they were *personally* responsible for the automobiles of the general staff and the general, too—and the cars did always get first-class service, not a fleck of dust—yes, and his brother-in-law had pledged him to secrecy and told him the attack was imminent. Imminent. He wasn't permitted, his brother-in-law, to let slip any of the information he acquired while carrying out his job; it was punishable with the death penalty, possibly, even; but he, the brother-in-law, of course, had told him, the milkman, everything.—He was shouting now. He hadn't said anything, he shouted, but the source was the general, the general himself, so help him God. He climbed back in behind the wheel. They'd be here tomorrow morning, the Huns, he shouted out the window. And he wouldn't like to be in the skins of such beautiful young women at that point, tomorrow, in the early morning, when the enemy crossed the country, raping everything in sight.—He got into gear, tapped the edge of the cap he wasn't wearing with his index finger, and drove off, to the turning area. When he returned, already driving at full throttle, he waved again and whirled up a cloud of dust, in which the women, coughing, vanished. When they were able to see again, the milk van was gone—from the dips beyond the horizon came two or three more toots of the horn—and my father could be seen, very small already, heading towards the edge of the forest. 'Karl!

Karl!' Clara shouted, waving her arms in the air. — 'Come back!' the women all shouted simultaneously, and as loud as they possibly could. 'Karl!' The latter turned, without slowing any, in his saddle, waved and disappeared into the trees. Clara put her arms down, and Nina burst into tears. For a while, the women — Clara, Nina, Jo, Hildegard, Rösli — all stood there, next to one another, looking across the meadows, until Rösli said, 'Now we've forgotten to buy milk' and they all went into the house. Me, too; I was with the women. — Almost a week later — he'd immediately written her a letter, to say he loved her, loved her terribly, and that she was to save herself and the child — my father got a postcard from Clara. (He'd been given extra kitchen duty as a punishment, and was sitting at a pile of potatoes he had to peel.) The picture on the card was a view of his home village, a section of the cobblestones. In the background, a few houses with their neat and tidy coffins, and the Black Chapel. Clara wrote that she was now here, with Nina and the child. Everyone had fled the town, everyone who could afford to. She'd even seen old Madame de Montmollin, apparently, standing in the back of her convertible, cursing the chauffeur below her for being stuck in the crowd. 'Of course, I would have much preferred to go to *my* relatives,' she wrote, in tiny handwriting, with which, if she'd had one, she could have written for well over a hundred years in *her* white book. 'But Nina says that to run away from the Germans to Italy would be as clever as trying to save yourself by climbing out of the lions' cage, and over into the tigers'. I don't believe that, my uncles would surely have protected me. But she can be so stubborn sometimes, Nina!' Yes, and Rüdiger didn't have any relatives, either; none, at any rate, who could have taken her in. 'Your uncle showed me your coffin right away,' Clara wrote. 'He wants to make one for the child too.' They were living — if my father managed to make it all out correctly—in a house at the end of the village, one with a single coffin at the door. 'The woman, whose house we're living in, remembers you. She says you didn't want to dance with her, back then, when you were together at some party at the inn. Her mother has just died—she'd a brother, too, but he fell into the ravine while chopping timber—that's why there's just her coffin there now, which she nonetheless lines up every morning, using a ruler and a spirit level to make sure it's completely parallel to the house. As if the house could shift overnight!—And now I have to close. Clara.'—The cook—the same one as at the training camp; he'd been posted to the Kessiloch too—pointed to the mountain of potatoes with his ladle. 'Do you think they're going to peel themselves?' he asked. My father shoved the postcard into his jacket pocket. 'It's from Clara,' he said. 'She's in safety, and Teddy is too.' He buttoned his jacket pocket again. 'I once read about a soldier who carried all of his loved one's letters in a pocket of his uniform over his heart. Just like me. That was during Napoleon's Italian campaigns. Under Napoleon, the postal service was first class. Much better than our forces' service. Express letters were delivered during the battles.'—'Really?' said the cook.—'She wrote to him every day, his little lady, and he piled his letters where I said he did, the soldier, and at the bridge at Lodi a bullet got him, right where his heart was, but it got stuck in all the paper. He'd a cracked rib, the soldier in love, nothing more than that, but his wife's declarations of love were left in shreds, every last one.' The cook nodded and mumbled something along the lines of: a woman who wrote letters was the last thing he needed. The point of women was to see to the table and the cowshed. My father took the knife, peeled a potato and threw it, across the kitchen, into the pot where the water was boiling and bubbling.

BEFORE LIGHTS OUT, as every other night, he took his white book—though his handwriting was almost as small as Clara's, it was already much more than half full, meanwhile—and the inkpot and the goose-quill from the locker and sat down at the bottom of his plank bed. Around him, his comrades were bustling about, in their underpants, barefoot, holding their toothbrushes. They were heading to the washing trough, returning from the washing trough, nudge-nudging with their elbows, noisy jokes, laughter. Fusiliers Schwan and Furrer were loudly discussing whether Bata shoes were made in Switzerland or Czechoslovakia. A few were already in their bunks and appeared, despite all the racket, to be sleeping. My father's immediate neighbour, a primary-school teacher from Gelterkinden, knocked the goose-quill out of his hand while trying to slip on his field-grey night shirt: no blot on the page, though; not a scratch. '*19.5.40 Letter from Clara,*' my father wrote, once he'd saved the quill from the hobnailed boots of a comrade, racing to the toilet. '*Kitchen duty for insubordination (the corporal asked me—it was to do with the dismantled gunlock I wasn't able to put together again—whether I thought he was stupid, and I said yes.) The Germans still aren't here yet. General mobiliza-*tion nonetheless.—In the ancien régime, *ladies'* vaginae *could speak, too. Not just their mouths. Often, the gentlemen would sit with their countesses and ducal lovers, having tea, and chatting to one another about an especially good* bon mot *of Madame de Pompadour or the Pope's last bull, while, simultaneously, from beneath their skirts—many-layered mountains of material—came a chattering and sniggering, the sense of which they didn't quite catch. At any rate, there was almost constant chat from down there. The many different mate-rials muffled the voices, but people sometimes thought they could hear their names, without knowing what the braying laughter beneath all the other skirts was all about.—The light! The light of the* dix-huitième, *you don't get light like that nowadays. The white horses that, with indescribable gracefulness, pulled golden coaches through bright parks. Shepherds showed shepherdesses, amidst the bleating herd, how to play the shepherd's pipe. The green, that pale sun, swans on the waters, yes, the horses and the swans and the ladies had the same necks. Heron flew across the azure sky, wild geese, beneath little white clouds. Porcelain deer springing towards distant woods, and in the clearings, here and there, a* chevalier *who, in a duel, stabbed his wife's lover to death in a courteous rage. — The world looked as if it were painted then, it* was *painted. — In all that bliss lived Diderot. Denis Diderot, my Diderot. Diderot wore a blue jacket, worn smooth at the elbows, and a small wig, sat at a roughly made table, looked over the roofs of Paris and wrote. Wrote and wrote and wrote. Sometimes I think I'm like Diderot, I am Diderot. He is me. We are the same. Mirror one another, each in his own era. — Diderot smoked, of course, when he was writing, and when he wasn't, the tobacco from back then, and he drank coffee. Diderot would do anything,* anything! *to get his hands on coffee. For a cartload of coffee from distant Brazil, he'd have sold his soul to the devil, and thrown in his wife for free. She was called Nanette, and was a pain. He coped with it, in his rapture, by not not listening when she ran after him like a talking shadow, giving him one of her lectures about the housekeeping money or him working so much. (In the case of the money, he was lucky in the end. Catherine the Great bought his library and let him keep it. She paid in cash. If only something like that would happen to me.) — He used goose-quills to write — what else was he supposed to use* à l'époque? *— and kept a flock of geese from the Limousin region where you got the best goose-quills: in order, at any hour of the day or night, to be able to keep on writing if, in the heat of the moment, he destroyed yet another quill. If a goose didn't have any feathers, was a case of only a few bristles in otherwise pink flesh, it ended up in the pot. — Diderot wrote like no other man or woman of his age, more boldly, more clearly, more freely and more impudently even* *than Monsieur de Voltaire whom he admired and didn't trust as far as he could spit. His words sparkled like stars, and his sentences flowed like a mountain stream through which anyone with two eyes in his head could see through the water to the stones at the bottom. Time was always tight, and always he was editing—under the greatest possible pressure and much too late in the day—an article for the* Encyclopédie. *Was formulating what he thought of* autorité, *which was to say:* nothing, *or at least not what the* ducs *and* archevêques *understood by it.—When the third volume was finished—weighty tomes—he'd only got as far as* catastrophe. *What a world. Obese lords messed around with their fawning courtiers while, under their noses, the corn was rotting and the peasants starved. Clerics were intimidating believers who were well past knowing what to believe, whom to believe. The local cleric, for instance? Their bishop? The King? They could choose only between dying soon, or there and then, on the spot. If, as the law required, they delivered the lords' share of the harvest to the castle, hardly a grain remained for them themselves; and if they rebelled, the Swiss in the King's Guards shot them to pieces. They flagellated themselves, wailed to the indigenous saints. Completely lost their faith. There was no avoiding it. In the end they'd be dead, and the end was coming closer with each year that passed. It was terrible, being a peasant. But it was also dreadful living as a* marquis, *as the King's* favourite. *To be the King himself. Rules of etiquette, even when you went to the loo, and in Versailles the rats were running through the corridors. Louis XV, when it was winter, went around with a red nose and his feet blue with the cold, as you couldn't heat the rooms that were as high as cathedrals. Not to mention the barons in the Vendée who had the rain pouring into their soup through the leaking roof.'*—'Lights out!' Fusilier Schwan roared, from far off. They were all, indeed, in their beds, meanwhile. Individual conversations still, ebbing away. My father went over to the light switch beside the door, turned off the light, flicked on his torch, and, by the light of it — a hint of light barely distinguishable from the darkness — returned to his bed. He sat down and carried on writing. '*To be Diderot, though!*' His handwriting was so small, he couldn't read it even when he held the glowing filament of the torch over it. '*In the eye of the typhoon of general unhappiness, to be merciless in naming the reasons for that misery: that had to be happiness itself. In a deadly era, Diderot was alive like no other and melted the ice of his epoch with his warm heart.*' My father was writing without being able to see what he was doing. '*He wouldn't have been able to do that elsewhere. Otherwise, anyone with a mind of his own and two legs fled to Britain, to Switzerland. Voltaire, Rousseau, everyone. Diderot stayed. He was incarcerated, he suffered, he signed humiliating confessions, but he was barely out again before he set about his work again. He wrote to d'Alembert and told him to get a move on and hand in his articles,* nom de dieu! *And it became clear to him that someone — no doubt, him again — would soon have to write the article about God.* Dieu. *His God was Reason. Write it as totally bluntly as that, though, and he'd end up in the dungeons of the Vatican or the Bastille. — In the evening, in the last light of the sun, he took out some especially beautiful paper, handmade, handmade by him, that gave off a scent like that of the Sultan's harem in the* Arabian Nights *as he wrote on it, and when the woman, for whom it was intended, raised it to her nose, to her lips, the lips that kissed his signature. Sophie loved Denis, and Denis loved Sophie, Sophie Volland, a delight, a stroke of good luck, even if they were both almost always, so to speak, ever apart. They saw one another so rarely that they sometimes thought each was an invention of the other. Between them lay green hills and vast plains, where messengers raced to and fro, couriers riding at full gallop that Diderot could never have afforded, and certainly not Sophie. And so they always used the horsemen of some enlightened high lord or other, or one who was at least a bit tolerant, of a* comte *or* abbé *who, for an extra fee, took the lovers' oaths with him and threw them to the loved one as he rode past. No, Diderot and Sophie were both so without malice and deception that their messengers, too, could do no other than dismount from their horses and, with the purest of hearts, deliver ten thousand kisses on the lips and then carry the return kisses back.'* The torch flickered but didn't go out. *'Sophie stood there, buried in the hussar representing her beloved. Just as Diderot, enraptured, accepted Sophie's kisses, though at times he'd have preferred a horsewoman to this batman, stinking of garlic. — Ah, Denis! Oh, Sophie! — Sophie slept with a locket between her breasts with a picture of Diderot, and Diderot only ever imagined Sophie when he was writhing in bed beside, or with, Nanette. Only Sophie, always Sophie, his one and only Sophie. — Unlike* vaginae, *there are no instances of* penes *with the ability to speak in the eighteenth century. The odd cry, perhaps, of Hey! Ho! Ah! from man to man. But back then, as nowadays, a* penis *didn't ever speak to a* vagina, *apart, of course, from Diderot's to Sophie's. — To bed at'* — my father held the barely shining light over the face of his watch — *'22.38.'* He blew on the ink, snapped the book shut, felt his way to his locker and put it under his underwear. He then took Clara's postcard from his pocket and tried to re-read it. But the torch now, finally, conked out, and so my father closed his eyes and was asleep before his head hit the pillow.

WHEN, A FEW WEEKS LATER, my father was discharged from the army, everything at home had returned to the way he'd left it. The Germans hadn't come, and all the women were back. Clara, Nina, Jo, Hildegard as well as Rösli. The frog, that is, me, was playing in his sandpit. Even Rüdiger was out on the terrace again, shouting orders, as if from a command bridge, at the mastiffs as they prowled around the garden. Hobby, too, was sniffing away at his favourite spots. That the ornamental fish weren't the ornamental fish that pre-dated the women's escape was something not even the fish knew. (Clara had forgotten the old ones, and so they'd starved to death, or suffocated. When the women got back, at any rate, they were belly-up, in the water. Clara had changed the water, wrapped one corpse in newspaper for reference and bought new ones that looked exactly the same, and the exact same number.) The weeds that had overgrown the dahlias and Michaelmas daisies, and even the larkspur and hollyhock, were weeded out. (Clara and Nina had spent days in the garden, scraping out even the moss in the cracks between the granite slabs in the path.) — My father, just this once, was walking not on the road but diagonally across what remained of the cornfield that had just been harvested. A shortcut. The house was shining, lit from behind by the huge burning sun setting in their garden. A black cube before a fireball. On the roof, rising into the already darker sky, the mast of their aerial. My father was walking quickly, anxious and excited, stumbling over the clods of earth such that his cutlery rattled around in his dishes and his bayonet kept hitting his leg. The steel helmet, at the top of his knapsack, bounced up and down. The light was dazzling him, but there was no doubt: there were shadows around the outside of the house, motionless, waiting. The women's shadows. Even when he screwed his eyes shut, and held both hands above them, he couldn't make out which was which. Were the silhouettes in front of the garage Jo and Hildegard? Or was Nina the one beside the water drum, and Rösli the one by the gate? The two rigid shadows, lurking next to the magnolia tree, were the mastiffs. Without a doubt. No doubt, either, that Clara was the patch of shadow beside a fire he couldn't see because its flames were being gobbled by the blazing sun. The smoke from it, though, was rising into the

evening-blue sky in blazing red clouds. Next to Clara, two
dots of shadow: the child and the dog. The dog and the child.
My father, Karl, danced and threw his arms in the air and
shrieked with delight, and, as if commanded to, the women
all began to move and vanished into the house. The mastiffs
did, too, as did Hobby—he'd been the bigger of the two
dots—and even the child that was slower than all the others,
and yet, almost immediately, was swallowed up by the black
cube. The sun went down, leaving a red glow over the horizon that paled quickly, and had completely disappeared by
the time my father reached the garden gate and—he was
wearing his hobnailed boots—made his noisy way up the
granite path. A blue dusk up to the front door of the house,
and hardly any more light as he rushed up the few stairs to the
apartment, stepped into the corridor and rushed across the
Afghan, or maybe Persian, rug in the living room, to get to his
writing corner, to his typewriter, where—still standing, with
his knapsack on his back, his carbine over his shoulder and his
cap on his head—groaning loudly, he wrote down everything
that had accumulated inside him in the months just past. (In
those nights at the tunnel portal, he'd translated into German
just about every sentence from French Literature he knew by
heart, and stored it all in his head.) And so he made a note of
Bérénice Racine's amorous sighs; the ending of *Candide*—
where the hero, and probably Monsieur de Voltaire too, wish
just to cultivate their gardens; that passage from Daudet's *Tartarin de Tarascon* in which Tartarin brags about hunting lions;
all of the beginning of the *Song of Roland* though he didn't really
like it, preferring the *Estoire de Tristan et Yseult*—which he did-
n't have in his head, though. For the beginning of Rimbaud's
Saison en enfer he'd found, trudging to and fro on the wooden
sleepers, his own words: 'Once, if I remember right, my life

was a feast, where all hearts opened, and the wine flowed.'
Whenever a page was full, at any rate, he tore it with an
assured flourish from the carriage and inserted a new one so
quickly that the clattering of the machine was uninter-
rupted. — Only once he could find nothing else in his head, his
gigantic skull, not a single word, did his fingers leave the keys,
and he flicked on the lamp — bright light across the desk — and
cast a quick glance at the page still in the typewriter — on it
were those lines from Molière's *Bourgeois gentilhomme* when
Monsieur Jordan is astonished to discover he's a genius
because, without realizing, he's been speaking in prose all
along — then he breathed in and breathed out — someone convalescing; someone done convalescing — and crossed the carpet
to return to the corridor. Clara was now standing there, or
always had been standing there. In black, quiet. My father
threw down his knapsack outside the loo, his cap onto the
shelf with the shoes, his carbine into the umbrella stand, and
then hugged his wife. 'Clara!' He held her close, and she
kissed him with pointed lips. 'Karl!' Reaching over his shoulder, she too now turned on the light: a yellow glass dome up
on the ceiling with dead flies in it. 'Och, Karl!' Her Karl let go
of her, laughed — 'Yes, I'm back!' — and now also hurled his
uniform jacket and his belt, complete with everything dangling
from it — bayonet, ammunition pouch, digging tools — into a
corner. Then he saw me, the child, and lifted me. 'Hello, Crocodile!' I was wriggling above him, screeching, and he kissed
me. I screamed with delight, and, once back on the floor, raced
into the nursery — 'Papa, look!' — and fetched the paper cigarette I'd rolled, on the tip of which I'd drawn coloured ash.
Red and black. 'Look, Papa!' I looked exactly like him when
I had it in my mouth! I wore cardboard glasses as well, that
looked exactly like his! When I got back to the corridor, my

father, though, was back at his desk and looking, lovingly, at his papers, pencils, rubbers and paper clips, his Sachs-Vilatte and Littré dictionaries. (Clara was kneeling on the Afghan or Persian rug, trying to fix the loose threads pulled by the nails on my father's boots.) My father, meanwhile, was stroking his two wooden sculptures from Africa: a stylized man with a long pointed head, and—at quite an angle to his body—an erection with a red tip; and a similarly abstract woman with a white V between her legs. He tapped the glass of the aquarium, and was pleased when the fish recognized him. He opened and closed the drawers in his desk—all except the top one—and sniffed at a tube of Pelikanol glue. 'Papa!' I called. He turned to me and reached into a drawer. 'Do you want a sweet?' Of course, I did, and I sucked it with the paper cigarette still between my lips and the cardboard glasses on my nose.—My father sank into the chair at the desk, a made-to-measure masterpiece by Herr Jehle, with a broad back-rest and two armrests; chair and father looked as if they'd come into this world as one. He, this father, now finally took off his hobnailed boots, pushing them well under the table, and groaned loudly, again. He was back.—That same evening, he invited all his painter friends and they all came, except the genius from the Weinland region, who was coughing up blood, meanwhile, and spent his days—pretty much his last—in the Mendrisiotto; and the wire sculptor who hadn't been demobbed yet and remained responsible for a few ventilation tunnels high above Göschenen. But Kirchner's pupil came, as did the Surrealist, the architect, the lady painter, too, who had her newly married husband with her, a black man with sparkling eyes whom she'd acquired during an adventurous escape from occupied France; and who, though they spoke to one another in French, was called Fenster and came from Düsseldorf.

Clara, Nina, Jo and Hildegard were, of course, also there.
Rüdiger, too, the only one still in uniform, looked in for a few
moments but went back upstairs almost immediately as he'd to
plead the next morning at an important trial. At midnight, even
Phil showed up, in an off-the-shoulder glittering dress she'd
worn to perform and with her new sweetheart, a saxophonist,
almost twice her size. They all—all, except Rüdiger, that is—
wanted to be together again, after weeks and weeks apart.
Their other goal was to finish off the Corton Clos du Roi bottles in the cellar, *completely* finish them and *that* same evening.
For if the Germans came at some point—and at some point
very soon, presumably—they certainly would, then the SS
shouldn't be allowed, at that point, to get their hands on these
splendours from Burgundy, that sacred place; first, as a matter
of principle; and second, because the master race thought a
Cröver Nacktarsch was the ultimate in pleasure, and wouldn't
begin to notice what they were knocking back. A dozen guests,
nineteen bottles. When morning broke, they were empty,
unlike the guests, of whom my father was the fullest, and who
showed his friends—glasses all over the floor, ashtrays, half-
eaten sandwiches—how he could walk on his hands. He was
happy. Things were, again, as they always had been.

BUT THEN THE WOMEN LEFT THE HOUSE. All of them, if not, all
at once. Not a single one was left, in the end. The first to go
was Jo, whom Rüdiger was pestering because she didn't pay
rent; and who sought shelter with her sister until Rüdiger
asked to see her papers, too. (My father grasped too late that
she was going, once and for all. He was at his desk, engrossed
in constructing a complex sentence that teemed with technical
terms relating to the art of warfare in the seventeenth century,

and waved, briefly, when Jo looked into the room and said that she was going. — Clara, in the kitchen, stood there, unable to say anything.) — Hildegard was next. She'd fallen in love — her feelings for Edwin Schimmel, such as they'd ever existed, had petered away — with a man with a zest for life called Rudi who, in the bar at the Singer, had his own bottle, and who earned his income by *not* going to the factory that belonged to his family and which his brother managed. Some sanitary installations or other, toilet bowls, bidets, bathtubs; Rudi observed the condition of his employment so strictly that he himself didn't know *exactly* what the firm produced. Nothing crucial to the war effort, profits were too low for that. — He met Hildegard as she was a friend of Phil Heymans, at whose feet he sat, every second evening. He slept a few times in Hildegard's one-room apartment but the bed was very narrow even for two in love — and it was a terribly long way to get there — so they switched things around, and Hildegard began to spend her nights at Rudi's apartment in the Old Town. She liked it — when she woke up in the morning, she could see, at an angle above her, the huge dial of the clock of St Peter's — and Rudi, too, liked more and more the woman he'd won by laughing — soon, he was utterly in love — with the result that, as early as the third morning, he proposed to her that she stay for ever. Hildegard, who was hardly awake, yawned and smiled and said yes and kissed him, and that very day they went backwards and forwards a dozen times between the house at the edge of town and Rudi's apartment; fooling around and laughing as they went uphill; carrying clothes, lamps and pans as they went back down again. As well as spoons, shoes, pictures. (My father missed this farewell, too. Was at his typewriter again, heard the coming and going but thought nothing of it, not even when Rudi and Hildegard crashed their way downstairs with a wooden chest, then sat on the bottom step, choking with laughter and the fright they'd got. Just some noise outside, he thought, as he tried to find a German equivalent for the expression *Partir, c'est mourir un peu*. Later, he ended up going out to the gate, after all; to the postbox. He was flicking through the post when Hildegard came up the slabbed path, without Rudi, but with a big bag in her hand. It was her final run, for the last odds and ends, so she put down her bag to kiss my father farewell but he shouted, 'I've got it! *Scheiden tut weh*!', raising his forefinger, and walking right past her. He thought, if anything at all, she was going shopping or on holiday for two or three days. Baffled, Hildegard watched as he went and called after him, 'Every farewell is a little death.' My father stopped mid-step, turned and looked at her, wide-eyed. He repeated the sentence in his head exactly as Hildegard had shouted it, and nodded. 'Thank you!' he said. But Hildegard was already on her way. She raised her free hand, without turning around. Her bag was so heavy that she was walking at a slant. My father threw his letters—advertising for Metzger shirts and something from the tax authorities—into the bin and went back into the house.—Clara was in the doorway, biting her lips.)—Then Rösli went. She ran down the stairs, crying, past my father, without seeing him. Astonished, he watched her go, her red coat flying in the air behind her. (On this occasion, too, it didn't occur to him that Rösli was going for ever. Rösli ran up and down the stairs a hundred times each day; not, however, having dissolved into tears first.—Clara was standing at the window, her eyes vacant; it wasn't even as if she especially liked Rösli.)—And finally, even Nina. It began with Rüdiger suddenly suffering terrible pains, a neuralgia, an infection, an allergy perhaps, too; at any rate, he and Nina and eventually even the doctor—a Dr Braun or Braunmann, called Browny by all his friends and therefore also by Rüdiger and Nina—were at their wits' end. Rüdiger ran, howling, round the house; the mastiffs howling after him, in his footsteps; and, on the floor below, in Clara and Karl's place, little Hobby howled, too, in solidarity. Browny decided, after none of the treatments had had any impact, to ease Rüdiger's pain, using morphine; small doses, that, week by week, were increased; and, eventually, were so large that Rüdiger was free of pain but came home from the consultations with his eyes flickering. He was happy again—Nina heaved a sigh of relief and yet was plagued by nightmares at night—but so radically happy that even his doctor realized what he'd done and stopped the morphine. Rüdiger, who, the next day, already, felt wretched, used all his remaining vitality to try and get hold of morphine. Black market, friends, it's even possible one of his sources continued to be Browny, only without a prescription and at higher prices. He injected his happiness drug, daily—if Nina didn't catch him, of course. (She wasn't to be deceived—not a lot, anyhow—and swore she'd do anything to make her sick husband well again.) He threw elaborate parties, reserved the entire Singer more than once, and gave Nina presents that left her feeling helpless. A watch full of diamonds, a pearl chain, shoes made of crocodile leather (a size too small) and underwear made of such delicate silk that Nina couldn't feel, and Rüdiger couldn't see, whether or not she was wearing it. One day, he bought her a 64-piece dinner service made of Langenthal porcelain; and, two days later, five cars: a Hotchkiss, a Citroën, an Adler, a Sunbeam and a used, but very well looked-after, Hispano-Suiza—though, in his garage, he'd a roadworthy Auto-Union Wanderer jacked up and, due to the war, no fuel rations whatsoever. Nina tried to persuade the car dealers as well as the Langenthal company that her husband was ill, that they should take the goods back. They did so, though not without deducting compensation of between five and twenty per cent. — But Rüdiger's bliss wasn't to last long, in any case. He was crashing, more and more frequently, from moods in which he thought he could conquer the world into hellish agony when he was convinced everyone wanted him dead. Nina, ahead of the rest. He pulled her hair, even hit her in the face once, leaving her with a black eye and a bloody nose. That day, she crept downstairs — Rüdiger could've prevented her; locked her in; and she didn't want Clara and Karl seeing her in this state — and went to Dr Braun, that is, Browny, to ask for help. He nodded, full of understanding, and said he'd impressed upon Rüdiger, time and again, that morphine and its withdrawal had a devastating effect. He gave her a handful of disposable syringes, powerful anaesthetics that, if faced with an emergency, she was to ram into Rüdiger somewhere. Into an arm, into his back, into his behind, it didn't matter where; and through all his clothing. Rüdiger found the syringes in her handbag that very evening, took one out, stared at it and roared, 'What are you injecting into yourself? Morphine?' and shot, before Nina could shout 'Stop!' the entire dose into his left arm. He fell to the ground as if struck by lightning, slept for ten hours, then woke with no memory of what had happened. — Nina was, as Browny anticipated, to need the injections on a few other occasions. Rüdiger, his hands already round her throat, fell straight to the carpet. — Apart from that, he continued to go to work — he was now the public prosecutor at the juvenile court; his efficiency in the military courts had accelerated his career on civvy street — he initialled files and spoke for hours to judges and defence lawyers on the phone but was no longer capable of preparing his summing up. He would stare at the blank page and ask Nina for help. So she read the files, squeezed out of Rüdiger what he made of the case—usually, he was swaying between acquittal and a life sentence—and then wrote the plea for him. She was in favour of mild judgements. (Rüdiger could address the jury, no problem, if you ignored the fact he'd sweat buckets and drink water by the litre as he did so.) Once, when Nina was working on a case that was   actually harmless—a youth had rolled stolen tyres down a hill with the Stations of the Cross and smashed the front window of a shop selling household goods—a woodpecker in a distant walnut tree irritated Rüdiger so much that he smashed his glasses to pieces on the edge of the table, and so Nina went into the garden and chased the woodpecker away, and whispered on the way back to Clara: could she not wait with the hoovering a bit, and could Karl not type a bit more quietly? Rüdiger was *thinking*. My father, who overheard her, hit the roof and roared, 'What about me? Am I *not* thinking?' Nina went back upstairs and my father carried on typing, raging. —Then Nina noticed Rüdiger had a girlfriend. A lover. (She wasn't the first other woman. Rösli, for instance, had run away because Rüdiger had entered her room, naked, and said, 'How about it, girl?'—or words to that effect.) Nina sobbed, initially, and bit her lips until they bled, then asked Rüdiger to at least bring this Lil—her name was actually Liliane—home with him. Anything but all this furtiveness. So Lil came round, the three of them ate together and drank wine—a Merlot—and later, in the living room now, several glasses of Cognac. Soon, all three were laughing quite a lot—close up, Lil was quite nice—and, suddenly, were lying in bed, in the bedroom, all three of them naked. Lil had bigger breasts than Nina; firmer hips, too; and a lot of pubic and underarm hair. Nina became very aroused, enjoying, frankly, Rüdiger kissing her and Lil watching. Perhaps she even reached a hand across and touched her breast or Lil did. She sighed. When Rüdiger suddenly left her alone, though, and his head disappeared between Lil's thighs—his hairy behind was up in the air—she jumped up and ran out of the room. She sat, naked, in the kitchen, on a stool, her legs crossed and a dish towel around her shoulders, listening to Rüdiger and Lil moaning their way towards their climax.—The next evening, Nina and Rüdiger were alone at the table—Lil had gone home, after all, late in the night, long after Nina had lain down on the sofa, unable to sleep, beneath a blanket—and Rüdiger bit into a fried potato and said, 'Too much salt!' Nina got up, took the serving dish with the potatoes and threw it out the window. While she was at it, she threw everything else out after it: the plates, the forks, the knives, the dish with the two steaks, the bowl full of cucumber salad, the glasses, the wine. The bread. The salt. (On the floor below, my father, Clara and the child were also at the dinner table. Objects came flying out of the sky, as if from space.) Rüdiger sat there, rigid. Nina closed the window gently and scurried out the door. (Her farewell, too, my father missed; or almost. For he'd been standing in the garden for the longest time already, his eyes to-ing and fro-ing, helplessly, between the sky and the ground. The sky was clear, immaculate. Scattered all over the grass: glasses and plates, in bits; a salt cellar. Among the blades of grass, slices of potato and cucumber. At the toe of his right shoe lay a steak. When he finally went up to the house, Nina was on her way down the road already, in a dress covered in flowers, her hair down. She was pulling a hand-cart behind her, with a suitcase and a few photo albums on it. A raincoat. Clara was standing, as white as chalk, at the garden gate, watching her sister go. Half an hour later, she was still there; an hour later, too; she only came back in once darkness had fallen.)

THE NEXT DAY, or a week later, my father heard Clara talking, even, or, especially, when she was alone. She was whispering to herself, whispering when she came down from the roof, whispering as she went down to the cellar. All day long, she rustled around the house, engaged in intense and barely audible dialogues with someone or other. My father stood in her way, tried—without success—to catch what she was saying, and asked: was everything okay? Clara fell silent, looked at him, shook her head. Went into the kitchen. Through the open door, he could then hear her again, discussing something in a choked voice with the pans. —One evening—winter had arrived, and it was snowing for the first time that year—Clara went to a concert of the Young Orchestra and came back— something she never did—by taxi. (That was something that barely existed, taxis, during the war.) Perhaps the snow was the reason. My father, already in his pyjamas, shouted, 'How was it?' and then carried on reading his book, Ernst Zahn's *The Thousand-Year-Old Road*, about which he wanted to write a—devastating, of course—review for the canton's bulletin for teachers, and which he discovered, while reading it, wasn't *that* idiotic. From the living room—he was sitting in the so-called warmth, a small room, the only one that was heated —he heard a groan that immediately stopped. A little scream, smothered by two hands, that had sounded different from the previous whisperings. Panic-stricken. So he put his book down on the little table where Clara piled the programmes of the Young Orchestra and a few other relics from her time with Edwin Schimmel, and went into the living room. Clara was sitting on the couch with a devastated expression on her face, staring at him, her eyes wide open, as if looking at her ruin. Did she recognize him? Her teeth were chattering—no wonder, it was icy cold—and she emitted that sound again. Like an animal howling, and she did, indeed, look — now, she raised her head and parted her teeth; perhaps to stop their chattering — more like a wolf and not like the Clara my father loved. She *was* a wolf. She'd been forced into a corner, some corner or other, and hissed at my father when he took a step or two towards her. He jumped back, holding up his arms. 'Clara?!' But now Clara was hammering her face with her fists: her teeth, her forehead, her cheek, her nose — that bled, immediately. The blood was running down her chin, and of course — because she reached for her nose — her hands, too, were soon smeared with blood. 'What's wrong?' my father asked, trying to catch her or perhaps to evade her. She was now raging round the room, and my father, withdrawing to his writing corner, reached for one of the African sculptures — the woman, as it happened — and raised it like a cudgel, or a fetish, in the air. (The child, me, was in the room now, too. My mother immediately shot over to me, her mouth wide open and full of red teeth. I screamed without making a sound and closed my eyes. Waited. But she stumbled, or her fist hit her on the chin such that she staggered backwards.) — My father brought her back to the couch, a whimpering bundle that lay there, crooked, biting into a cushion. A tubular steel armchair had been overturned, the coffee table knocked over and the painting by Kirchner's pupil — *L'après-midi bourgeois* — had crashed to the floor. Over the bright green lawn, where Hobby, the dog, had been running, was her hand-print; black, almost. Her teeth were clenching the cushion she'd bitten into, and she was shaking her head as if she could get rid of it that way. She was howling, too, and finally my father noticed she was saying something. 'What?' he asked. She let go of the cushion, her face fell onto it, and she said, 'I can't take it any more.' It sounded muffled, choked. Her shoulders were shaking. She couldn't take it any more. 'Should I call a doctor?' my father asked. 'A doctor, I should—' He spotted me. 'Look after Mama,' he said, pushing the wooden statue into my hands. 'I need to call Dr Massini.' He disappeared into the corridor. So I looked after Clara, after my mother. She turned her face to me—dried blood above her lips—got up, supporting herself with both hands on the couch, and came dizzily, with her arms extended, towards me. Her face hovered—I was as big, as small, as any four-year-old—high above me. She bared her teeth—or was that a smile?—and her lips twitched. I dropped the African fetish-woman and charged towards my father who had just returned to the room. 'Yesyesyes,' he said, taking Clara by the elbow, and leading her back to the couch. He gave her the cushion. She pressed it against her stomach. They sat there like that until the doorbell rang and Dr Massini came in, a fur cap on his head and a trail of snow falling from his boots. 'What's the matter with us, then?' he asked. 'What's the matter with us, then?' He raised Clara's eyelids; she was quite calm now. Dr Massini gave her an injection, nonetheless, then made a call, took Clara's arm, and they all left the room, and—after rumbling around in the dark corridor for a while—the apartment. Dr Massini was wearing his cap again, or he hadn't taken it off. Clara had put her coat with the fur collar over her shoulders, and had the wooden African in her hand. My father had on sturdy shoes. He was also smoking again, and wearing his winter coat. That said, beneath it, you could see his pyjama trousers. —At the garden gate, he turned back. The child, me, was at the door of the house. He raised and dropped his hands, then climbed into the doctor's car, an Opel Olympia with a wooden carburettor at the rear. The thing blocked his view when he wanted to look out the rear window as Dr Massini tried to turn in the snow. He was turning the steering wheel like mad. The car swayed to and fro, Clara's body echoing its every movement. Dr Massini then accelerated so much that the wheels began to spin. But, after a few scary moments, the tyres gripped and the car lurched, more or less on course, along the road. Dr Massini looked at Clara as if hoping for applause. But Clara was whimpering to herself. — Just before the car dipped into the steep part of the road, my father looked at the house once more. His son was standing in the light of the door-way, petrified, tiny. Snowflakes were streaming from the sky.

MY FATHER RETURNED THAT SAME NIGHT — the child, me, was at the door, with a layer of snow, the thickness of your thumb, on his head — and took up position, in his hat and coat — snow on them, too — at that window where Clara otherwise stood, looking across at the forest. Now, he was staring. He wanted, perhaps, to see what she had seen. It was only: now, it was night, and snow was still swirling from the sky, a white storm, turning black further back, the flakes flying from above and below and diagonally. The snow on his hat and coat melted, leaving my father standing in a puddle. Next to my father was the child, also melting, and — like him — looking, but not — I was small — out the window but at the central-heating pipes. I pressed against them, and pushed my right hand into my father's left; he squeezed it, but didn't look away from the win-dow. — The snow was sweeping across the plain as if fleeing, darting sideways, rising in columns, coming down in thick packs, crashing onto the field. — Later, my father went into the kitchen — the child with him — and opened a tin of white beans in tomato sauce, and he and the child ate them, cold, sharing a fork. This time, I took a stool with me and, standing next to my father, could now see outside. The snow had stopped streaming from the sky, and when day broke — hours later, hours in which my father had smoked twenty or thirty cigarettes — the plain lay there like a sea, with soft white waves; the distant forest might have been a rocky reef. Quietness, just the breathing of father and child, and the creaks of the heating. Here and there in the snow, the tracks of hares or wild boar. The sky as white as the snow, such that everything out there was sky, or snow. — My father and I were still standing there like that when it was daylight and Frau Holm came, who did the washing once a week, and whose day for it, coincidentally, was today. Thursday. She asked where was Clara, and, getting no answer, set about her work. When the washing was washed and the kitchen cleaned and the husband and child of her employer were still looking out the window, she said, 'That's me then!' and left. — Hobby had also been missing from the previous evening. The child and, in any case, my father checked all the tracks in the snow to see if Hobby might have made them. But he hadn't; Hobby, who had hair like a mop, would have left a broader track. 'There, Hobby!' I called nonetheless, pointing to a distant, Hobby-sized patch in the snow. My father opened the window, clapped his hands, and Hobby flew, cawing, into the air. My father closed the window, and said, 'Dogs can't fly.' — 'When will she be back?' I said, after a long while. My father said, 'Never again,' and began to cry. 'Not the way she was, anyway.' The tears — he hadn't shaved — got stuck in his stubble and dripped individually from his chin. 'Papa,' the child, me, said, not crying himself, though: 'Hobby, you know what she's like. She'll get through anything.'

SOMEHOW OR OTHER, my father was then permitted, or obliged, to visit Clara, after all. (She was in the Psychiatric

Clinic in Münchenbuchsee.) He dressed the child in the bright trousers, the nice pullover, the white socks and its Sunday shoes. He himself was in his hat, glasses, cigarette, coat. (He never wore anything else; in summer, a jacket, a white shirt, a claret, badly knotted tie.) They took the train to Berne, on the wooden third-class benches, of course, and pointing out to one another the dogs, cats, cows, that whizzed past. Everything that was alive. I, the child, was much better at it. He wasn't quite with it, and took a pile of wood for an ox and an old tree for a farmer. They laughed a lot. Just before Berne, the train — slowly, as if it wanted to drag everything out — went over a bridge with bright blue water beneath it. Ducks in the distance. The child shrieked with delight. — In Berne, they went — because, if they were visiting Clara, they could kill that bird, too, with one stone — to a famous child psychologist. To Hans Zulliger, perhaps; he was wearing a white coat, at any rate, and spoke Bernese dialect. He examined the child because Rüdiger had told my father it was mad. It had stuck his tongue out at him. 'It's mad!' Rüdiger screamed, pointing his long arm at me. And yet it was *him* who had thrown the dishes out the window and bought all those cars. Our birthdays, on the other hand, were on the same day, and the child, me, beat itself on the forehead in its sleep with such a regular rhythm that you could've used it as a metronome. It would beat out something like an andante with the back of its right hand, always; the whole night long, if you let it. When it was awake, it twisted its hair into knots it then tore out with a painful tug. It sucked the thumb of its right hand so hard that the thing, literally, began to soften. It stood, petrified, in the corners of rooms, its eyes focused hard in the distance, and got a terrible fright if Clara or its father came into the room. When it wasn't rigid, it whistled, not like a bird but with

pursed lips: entire concerts, the violin part from Beethoven's
Concerto, all three movements, or Ravel's Bolero with many
more repetitions than the piece, in any case, has. And yet it
was a bird, the child, for, like it, a bird says with its singing
too: here I am, I exist, this is my space. I am well. — My father, at Dr Zulliger's, had to leave the room, and the child
thought that was him gone for ever. He was sitting in the waiting room, though, flicking through *Nebelspalter*. Really badly
drawn caricatures of gigantic Swiss men — he recognized the
dairyman caps — licking the behind of a little Hitler. Then the
door opened again, and his son came rushing at him. Was
clinging at his arm as if he never wanted to let go. Dr Zulliger
told my father his son wasn't mad, not at all, and my father,
who hadn't thought so, but had allowed himself to be intimi-
dated by Rüdiger, stood up, wiped the sweat from his brow
with a handkerchief and said, 'Thank you, thank you very
much, and now we have to move on a department. Come on,
Tom Cat.' — The Münchenbuchsee Clinic was surrounded by
greenery. A large garden, a park full of flame-like flowers and
gigantic trees. Perhaps there were also peacocks. Across a
gently sloping lawn, a white figure floated up to us, her head
at an angle, smiling, her hands outstretched. Clara. Her feet
barely touched the ground. She hugged Karl and the child,
without any force, body-less. Her gaze slipped past them, off
into the distance. But she was feeling better, yes, she was feeling better. She nodded, without her eyes joining in. She was
being given electroshocks, daily. The child looked up at its
mother. She smiled and put a hand on its head, and then she
and my father walked up and down the lawn, arm in arm. The
child chased a peacock, then fled from it when it did a sudden
about-turn and opened its beak. Karl, my father, her husband,
said to Clara that they had to be patient, they both had to be

very patient. Everything was okay at home. Frau Holm was still coming, yes. He longed for her to be home again. Clara smiled, said she did too. — That Hobby had never come back, he didn't tell her. Maybe she'd turn up again, before she came home. — Then he and his son took the train back. Again, just after Berne, the Aare was as blue as the South Seas.

MY FATHER, Rüdiger, and two big thin men, one of them wearing the uniform of a lieutenant of the guards up at the fortress, and the other a grey jacket with leather patches at the elbows, were standing at the inner garden gate — there to prevent the mastiffs from getting out — astonished by the sea of flowers, stretching to far beyond the walnut tree, and only stopping at the fence at the rear where the farmers' crops took over. Phlox, larkspur, daisies, irises, lady's slipper, peonies, monk's hood, alpine anemones, poppy, star flowers, sweet pea. Grasses, too, and reeds. Thousands, thousands upon thousands of flowers and calyxes in every colour; everything that Clara had planted and sown. — The two men had come by bicycle, and both had clips at the bottom of their trousers to stop them catching in the chain. They were sweating buckets, and had been tasked with putting the so-called Wahlen Plan into practice in the south-west sector of town. (The thing had been worked out by Friedrich Traugott Wahlen, commissioned by the entire Council of Ministers and the Army High Command, and envisaged every square metre in the country being planted with grain, potatoes or white cabbage in order to achieve the greatest possible self-sufficiency in terms of supplies. Ideally, every evening, every Swiss person would have his own carrot.) The garden was, of course, larger than every permitted limit — the Federation was planting even traffic

islands and handkerchief-sized front gardens with a handful
of grains of rye—and required professional farming. The big
thin one in uniform screwed up his eyes, held an arm well out
and raised his thumb. He was estimating the total yield of the
future plantation. 'You can list it as an *agricultural business*—
small, or as a *horticultural business*—large,' he said to the thin
big civilian who was waving around a bundle of forms and
taking notes. A gust of wind caused the forms and all the flowers to dance. My father, Rüdiger and the two men bathed for
a few moments in a wondrous fragrance. The civilian, thin-
and-big one was so enchanted that he didn't notice a few of his
papers flying across the garden, like birds. Bees were buzzing,
butterflies fluttering. Heat in the blue air, almost summer
already. 'We've no option,' the uniformed big-and-thin one
then said, though to Rüdiger more than my father as Rüdiger
was the proprietor, 'but to commandeer the entire area of cul-
tivable land, and have it farmed by members of the army.
Unless, that is, you can guarantee its cultivation by an expert.
Who, here in this house, would be capable and willing?' My
father looked at Rüdiger, Rüdiger at my father; both, agreed
for once, were about to shake their heads and reply 'Very certainly not me' or 'I am a fully qualified lawyer, Sir, not a
farmer,' when from behind them a voice said, 'Me!' Clara.
There she was, Clara, back from the clinic, as radiant as life
itself, with her little suitcase in one hand and her coat with the
fur collar over her other arm. 'I'll do the garden!' She beamed
first at the uniformed official—who blushed and touched the
peak of his cap—and then at the civilian, until, his eyes deep
in hers, he held the forms out with an ecstatic grin. She signed
them—a queen casually signing a state treaty—smiled now for
Rüdiger and my father, too, and began to walk—parting the
flowers as she went—towards the shed. My father followed

two or three steps behind, his arms outstretched; then he stopped. Her dress was bobbing up and down, and, halfway there, she bent and walked the rest of the way barefoot, her red high heels swinging from her left hand. She disappeared into the shed (her small suitcase and coat had remained at the gate) and came back out, not even a minute later, with mountain boots on her feet and wearing a blue gardener's apron. In her hand she'd a hoe with which she immediately went at the flowers with such force that all four men took a joint step backwards. Wide-eyed and open-mouthed, they watched the raging farmer whose blows with the hoe were sending flowers spinning everywhere. Eventually, the one in uniform was the first to close his jaws again. 'That'll be that then, or what do you reckon, Heiner?' he said. Heiner, the civilian, nodded and said, 'Looks like it, Peter.' Both turned to my father and Rüdiger, who were still staring at Clara. 'Enjoy the rest of your day,' they chorused, and headed for the gate. They got onto their bikes, and soon their heads—they chose the track across the fields that led along the garden—were hovering beyond the sea of flowers in which Clara was standing, flinging larkspur into the air. They rang their bells, and Peter, the one in uniform, again tipped his cap. — My father sat down at his desk once more. He wiped the sweat from his brow, lit a new cigarette and cleaned his glasses. Out the window he could see Clara, his Clara. She was healthy again! She felt well! She was cured! She raked up the flowers she tore out. Then she burnt them. She turned over the earth. She broke it up. She created beds. She stamped out little paths. She sowed seeds. She planted seedlings. She hammered poles into the ground. She fetched and carried watering cans. She weeded. My father, typing with the index finger of his right hand, waved to her with his left. But she was running over to the

shed now, to fetch bast; and didn't wave back. Perhaps because of a reflection on the outside of the window. — By the
time the two big thin officials returned — Peter was wearing
his uniform; Heiner, though, was in a tartan shirt — the former wild flower garden had become a well-ordered plantation, a vegetable garden with young beans, peas, onions,
carrots, and from a kind of metal rucksack Clara was spraying a garish blue fog over everything and anything; herself,
too, and the child and the two officials. 'For a business of this
size, you need three other colleagues,' Peter roared so loudly
that even my father, far away in the house, understood him.
'Do you have them?' — 'Yes,' Clara roared back. 'I'm doing
the work of four people.' Peter and Heiner nodded, noted
their findings in their papers and withdrew. — My father, now
Clara was back to normal, had excessive plans again. If he
wasn't making progress with the translation of *Grand Meaulnes*
by Alain-Fournier, and hadn't a feature article or a polemical
piece on the go for the *Nachrichten*, he was writing a textbook
on the French language. (In his feature articles, he invented
little everyday occurrences, for example, a dog bites a postman and he bites it back; his polemical pieces called politicians influenced by the Nazis, sadistic military types, or idiotic
censors exactly that: idiotic, sadistic and influenced by the
Nazis — with the result that they didn't actually ever get past
the advance censorship of the newspaper's editor.) The textbook was called *Pas à Pas*. Step by step, the pupils were to
learn the peculiarities of the French language on a pleasura-
ble stroll from chapter to chapter, for example, the correct use
of the *imparfait* and of the *passé défini*: '*La belle princesse* était as-
sise dans sa chambre et tricotait *paisiblement, lorsque tout d'un coup
un brigand* entra.' The continuously, and therefore in the
imparfait, sitting and knitting princess was threatened by the

robber who appeared suddenly, and—therefore—in the *passé défini*. He wanted to harm her. But, at that very moment, Guignol, the clown figure, turned up, he too, of course, in the *passé défini*, and thrashed the robber for such a long time and so continuously with his rattle that, in the course of this rain of blows, the *passé défini* gave up and made way for the *imparfait* again. Why the classical, happily-ever-after, final sentence of all French fairy tales since the days of Perrault nonetheless read '*Et ils vécurent heureux jusqu'à la fin de leurs jours*', not even my father could explain and so his story ended without it.— There were cartoons, too, in which secondary-school teachers slipped on banana skins, or massive fathers begged for mercy as their tiny sons got them in a headlock.—Clara was still sweeping up and down the garden, between beans that were climbing and semi-ripe tomatoes.—In Hildegard's attic room now lived a Herr Feix. Herr Feix had crossed the Rhine somewhere near Dornbirn, in Austria, and owned nothing but the clothes on his back, a very creased suit made of Oxford flannel and buckskin shoes, the soles of which were full of holes. He spent the entire day in Clara's kitchen—Clara was in the garden, of course—with an apron over his suit. His idea was to remove the water from potatoes or apples—in principle, however, his plan had to work for all types of fruit and vegetables—such that these, now dehydrated, became a powder he could turn back into mashed potato or apple purée by adding water. He boiled and steamed and cut and stirred and cooled and weighed and noted his results in tables, and, every evening, with fearful pride, served the results of his research to my father, Clara and the child. My father ate and said, 'That tastes wonderful, Herr Feix!' whereas Clara shook her head and shovelled the food into the bin. The child, me, didn't eat the stuff either. (After the war, Herr Feix returned to his

homeland, to Innsbruck, and was given back his factory that
had been 'aryanized' by the Nazis. He sat in his director's
chair again, the leather of which had tears and cracks in it
because, for seven years, an SS man had been sitting on it. He
noted and took on board that someone else had been more successful at inventing freeze-dried mashed potatoes or had been
quicker to patent it. He bought himself a new suit and new
shoes—not as fine as the old ones; there wasn't any flannel
from Oxford or buckskin from deer any more—and produced
once more the gelling agent that had already been the market
leader before the war.) When he wasn't doing that, Herr Feix
helped Clara in the garden—the only one in the house to do
so—and carried crates full of kohlrabi for her, or crouched between green leaves collecting Colorado beetles in a bucket.—
Another constant guest in the house—he, too, a refugee, albeit
not a Jew—was older than Herr Feix, nearly old already, a
delicate man called Alexander Moritz Frey, known to everyone
as Amf. 'Amf has forgotten his brolly again.' 'Amf doesn't like
cauliflower, surely you know that.' 'Heat the kitchen, too, or
Amf will freeze to death as we eat.' On the night of a new
moon, he'd rowed across Lake Constance, into Switzerland,—
he was a non-swimmer, suffered from night blindness, had a
weak heart—and, in pre-Nazi Germany, had been an almost
famous author. In the country he'd fled to, where, of course,
German was actually spoken and read, no one had heard of
him. He hadn't heard of anyone either—apart from Hermann
Hesse and Thomas Mann, who, when he wrote them a letter,
reacted in guarded fashion—and didn't understand Swiss
German. Every greeting he took to be a threat, and every
question part of an interrogation. He did have a residence per-
mit but one that forbade him to leave the general area of Wallisellen and to follow a profession in any form; even to write

and to publish. (The authorities, as advised by the Writers'
Union, ensured that books, newspapers and magazines
remained the preserve of the local producers.) And so Amf's
excursions into town—and he wasn't entirely wrong in saying
this—were dangerous expeditions, from which he tried,
sitting pale-faced in the tubular steel chair in the living room,
to recover—until the moment came when he began to tremble
again because the return journey beckoned. Actually, he was
always trembling. He didn't dare take the tram, though my
father had pressed a multi-journey ticket into his hand, and,
instead, walked the whole way with those slow shuffling steps
of his, an hour and a half to get here, an hour and a half to get
back. He thought he wouldn't be checked if he walked slowly;
and couldn't walk any faster, anyway. (On one occasion,
though, a policeman did want to see his papers, when Amf
was standing right on the border of the district of Wallisellen.
The policeman nodded and gave him his ID back.)—With my
father he drank coffee and grumbled about Hesse and Mann.
What stupid books *Steppenwolf* and *Königliche Hoheit* were. He
recited poems by August Stramm and Else Lasker-Schüler that
he knew by heart, though his own writing was completely different. (His writing was delicate, hesitant, sad.) My father gave
him money and introduced him to the editor of the *Nachrichten*
who, though he always returned his polemical pieces, didn't
think much of the authorities' decrees muzzling the freedom
of speech and so published Amf's prose sketches and book
reviews under a local-sounding pseudonym. Amf then lived
off the fee, twenty francs, for a month.—The most frequent
guest, however, wasn't an emigré, nor a Jew, but a Bernese.
He came from Bümpliz, to be precise, and looked like a cham-
pion wrestler. Sawdust on the seat of his pants, clods of earth
on his shoes. He'd a skull like a boundary stone, bristly hair

and hands that, when he washed dishes—he'd insist after every meal, after carefully counting out his ration vouchers and placing them on the table, on helping Clara with the washing up—broke the stem of every glass he touched and split plates in two. His name was Züst, Albert Züst, and he was a farmer. His business, however—a model farm of almost Argentinian proportions—wasn't his at all but belonged to his wife. Her, rich; him, poor; that was the role division in their marriage. Both were on their feet from dawn to dusk; he was paid a wage for his work by her. With this money—late in the evening, when the manure had been dealt with—he ran a publishing house, Albert-Züst Verlag. Of course, it was their love of books that brought him and my father together. (He developed, however, an admiration that grew from month to month for Clara's agricultural achievements as he now really knew something about it, and would've needed at least five colleagues for her business to keep it in similar shape.) Züst, who, in real life, wrestled down bulls and lifted tractor wheels with one hand, loved the small and light when it came to books; as well as the non-conformist, the anarchic and the contrary. Something ugly could be, for him, something beautiful. My father, of course, knew of entire libraries that should be included in his list right away. Some of the books didn't exist yet, had to be created by him; others did, but only in remote imprints and very foreign languages; and a pile of manuscripts the length of his arm could go to print *hic et nunc*. Züst was enthusiastic. He was enraptured most by the *Ulenspiegel*, my father's pet project, too, of course; and so it was done first. *Ulenspiegel. The Legend and the Heroic, Happy Adventures of Ulenspiegel and Lamme Goedzak in Flanders and Elsewhere* by Charles De Coster. They went through it, page by page—at Züst's request, he *loved* his books, and wanted, by editing them, to

have written them himself, so to speak, so very like my father
in that respect—and, of course, each time Züst objected to a
comma or an old-fashioned adjective, my father first went red
in the face, then into a maniacal rage, then roared, slammed
the door behind him, stomped round the magnolia tree three
times, came back in and agreed to the change.—He travelled
to Berne, to Bümpliz, where Züst showed him the farmyard,
the cows, the pigs, the geese, the lean meadows, the rich meadows, the cornfields, the children, his wife. She, in traditional
costume—a Bernese costume, with lots of frills and ribbons,
and a hat like a black peacock fanning out its tail—nodded to
my father and disappeared among high beanpoles. Again,
Züst said, yes, that's the way it was, that was the deal, there
wasn't a single rappen of hers invested in the publishing company, and he, with the books, had to budget differently from
what she did in the agricultural business, where she could
absolutely agree to expensive machinery and costly growing
methods as her farm was to be better managed and more eco-
nomical than all the others—and it was, as well—yielding
more, even, than her father's, who was the king of the Emme
Valley, and the Federal Agricultural Office had long since
adopted her norms, and not the other way round.—Albert
Züst couldn't afford a two-tone cover for the *Ulenspiegel* but
had designed one nonetheless—using a woodcut by Franz
Masereel—at the centre of which a glowing sun set behind
the silhouette of a dying warrior. And so he and my father sat
up all night, twice, on the floor of the cellar that was the publishing company, using watercolours to paint the sun red,
blood-red, for the whole print-run, one thousand and five
hundred copies.—For the *Ulenspiegel*, Züst had chosen an
especially beautiful endpaper, paper made from corn, grained,
and with a yellowy shine, that began to curl, however, if the

Central Meteorological Office, in its forecast, even considered the possibility of it clouding over. It couldn't take any humidity, not a drop of water, and the brand-new books, when they reached the booksellers, all looked like old corrugated cardboard. The booksellers complained, of course. Züst sent them a leaflet, advising them to press the books with an iron, ideally, immediately before a customer was about to turn to them. — Next, Züst printed — this time on corn-free paper — *The Story of the Life of Lazarillo of Tormes and his Sufferings and Joys, as Told by Him Himself, and Complete with its Sequel*, a forgotten classic of the sixteenth century — the *Lazarillo* was the first-ever picaresque novel — which my father, who didn't have Spanish, had translated from the Castilian of the time. (Perhaps that's why he used a pseudonym. Urs Usenbenz. He used it again a few times later; once, for instance, for his translation of poems by Melachos of Corinth — ancient Greek, my father knew — in which beautiful women slowly opened their legs) — Then it was one after the other: *The Kunkel Gospels* — older than the *Lazarillo* and just as ribald; Daudet's *Tartarin de Tarascon* and *Tartarin's Journey to the Swiss Alps* and *The Crafty Little Mice*, the relief plates for which — red and blue — had slipped throughout the entire print-run; and, finally, a teenage novel my father had written on the tram, on his way to school, called *Vinzi and the Black Hand*. In the case of *Vinzi*, *his* name was on the cover, and not Urs Usenbenz, perhaps because it was about the little Karl he'd once been, his heroic deeds, that, above all, involved putting the local policeman, Rüti, in his place. (My father made countless clay Rütis that he painted different colours — red face, black snout, green shako — that were all over the house, and, like garden gnomes, beside the mailbox and in front of the dog compound; and that — because the clay hadn't been fired — collapsed after a short while and were cleared away by Clara.) — Coincidentally, the day the *Wehrma-cht* capitulated in Stalingrad, Herr Feix *and* Amf *and* Züst were in the house. It was icy-cold outside — not even Clara was in the garden — and they were all sitting, bunched close together, in the 'warmth'. They flung their arms round one another's necks and laughed and felt pleased, and, as if the wonderful news were a command, the painters turned up, one after another. (Perhaps they'd discussed it between them.) They, too, squeezed their way into the room that wasn't much bigger than the double bed in it. So they settled on the bed — a few were sitting on the windowsills, or on Clara's ladies' writing desk — and kissed the people closest — man or woman, it didn't matter — and clapped one another on the shoulder. They were all glowing. Now, they regretted being scaredy-cats and drinking, back then, all the bottles of Corton Clos du Roi. They'd to settle for a Féchy, in litre bottles, but the day was so splendid that their stomachs would have accepted even vinegar. For the first time — the first time! — the *Wehrmacht* had been beaten, a crushing defeat! They drank to Stalin's health, then to Molotov's and Voroshilov's and Malenkov's, and to that of every single solder in the heroic Red Army. It was the beginning of the end for the Nazis! They now had a chance, after all, of escaping all that. They sang every song that came into their heads, 'Stenka Rasin' and 'Veronika, der Lenz ist da', and, finally, the 'Internationale'. They sang at the tops of their voices, all of them. The lady painter, whose hair was shining even redder. The Surrealist, whose *nose* it was, that did that. The lady painter's husband, blacker than ever. The architect. The wire sculptor. My father. (Rüdiger, lured downstairs by the joyous noise, and who, graced with a wonderful voice, sang the bass solos in the chamber choir of the Young Orchestra, at first stood, silent, in the doorway. Then, however, the enthusiasm of the others swept him away, and he began to bellow so powerfully that Clara, standing in front of him, had to duck.) Clara had a delicate soprano voice. Züst was roaring. Herr Feix glowed quietly to himself, and hummed, his eyes closed. Even Amf was cawing the 'Internationale' with a low, cracked voice: its call for the final struggle, to unite the human race.

ON 11 MARCH 1944, the elections for the town council took place. The seven members of the Federal Council had to be elected too; or rather, confirmed, for only the previous office holders were standing as candidates: four Social Democrats and three Bourgeois. Their re-election was a formality. Seven members, seven candidates. That said, standing for election to the town council—one hundred and thirty mandates were available—alongside the well-known parties, was a 'List of Labour' that, a month earlier, no one had heard of. Not even those on the list. It wasn't even a party; rather, a case of men coming together—women were to be excluded from politics for many years still—and among them, anyone could recognize, without difficulty, some of those communists whose party had been banned in 1940, and remained banned. But the 'List of Labour', submitted at the last minute, was permitted to stand; the political climate, now that no one doubted the Nazis would be defeated, had changed. Only the three or four top dogs of the old Communist Party had to be removed from the list: if the authorities had permitted their candidacy, they could no longer have in any way justified the party remaining banned. The architect was made No. 1 on the list, and could hope to be elected. For Kirchner's pupil, in fourth place, the task seemed already more difficult.—In order to submit a full list, the architect had implored my father to stand also. He had little desire to—a politician was really not something he wanted to be—but when the architect promised him nineteenth place on the list, he agreed. Below him was only a typesetter called Wälti, only old enough to vote by a matter of days and still waiting for his voice to break. The architect also persuaded my father to speak at a 'List of Labour' election meeting at the Volkshaus. He was the specialist for questions relating to education. The room was full to bursting—a good two thousand men and women—and, when my father climbed the little staircase up to the rostrum, he could see just as many raised fists. Hot faces. Howling. Shouting. Up on the stage, his glasses immediately steamed over, and the lights dazzled him so much that he was glad—as he rowed with his hands—to get to the edge of the lectern. He took his glasses off, wiped them clean and shouted—in order to say something—'Comrades!' Thunderous applause. He was still squinting blindly and so again shouted, 'Comrades!' The applause was even greater. He put his glasses back on but then he couldn't make out a letter of his script; the light was glaring too much. So he let his script be just that: a script—and spoke with a voice that, with each sentence, was becoming more certain, into the black hole in which his audience was concealed. He demanded a school reform, *the* reform of all schools. Everything had to change. Be better. Smaller classes, much smaller. More and better-trained teachers. Education authorities who knew something about education. New teaching materials, completely new. The children had to be taught to be democrats, to be partners of the teachers and with equal rights. All existing school buildings, proper prisons often, should be torn down and replaced by new buildings full of light and sun. 'Many teachers, comrades, are dafter than their pupils!' my father shouted, deviating completely from the script he'd written the previous evening and that the architect, shortly before the event, had toned down, by deleting all the adjectives, to something reasonably objective. 'Much dafter!' The audience went wild. My father didn't know whether he was allowed to bow, and so raised his fist. — The election was a triumph for the Left. The Social Democrats got almost as many votes as all the bourgeois parties put together, and became the largest party. Above all, however, the 'List of Labour' — from a standing position — secured eighteen seats. (A prediction within the party — that even the architect considered optimistic — had hoped for three, at best four.) A few more votes, and even my father would have got in. — He was waiting for the result at their usual table in the Ticino, with the lady painter, the Surrealist, and the typesetter, whose voice cracked even more when he heard the first results of the count, and who, with each glass, reckoned he'd even more chance of being elected, after all. My father wasn't drinking any less than Comrade Wälti but was becoming more and more quiet. — At about midnight the architect phoned with the result. Luigi took the call — the Thieves' Den was *his* place — and his eyes, as all the customers could see, grew rounder and rounder. '*Sì,*' he said. '*Ho capito.*' He removed the receiver from his ear, looked into it, put it back to his ear and said, '*Sì! Sì! Sì!*' His whole skull was now burning red and he was sweating. '*Il popolo vincerà,*' he whispered and hung up. He clenched his fist. '*Dio mio!*' He drank a beer — that was on the counter and intended for the lady painter — in a oner. By the time he got to the regulars' table, he'd forgotten all the figures already. A lot of votes, at any rate, a great lot. A landslide victory! All the candidates had been elected! More than all of them! Everyone, here in this room, had they been on the 'List of Labour', would have been elected. A historic day! — To celebrate his entry into politics, the typesetter stood a round for everyone at the table that cost him his entire wage as an apprentice; and my father ordered, in addition, an eau-de-vie; a double. Later, there was a knock at the back door of the pub that had been nominally closed for two hours already and, to the outside world, appeared to be in the dark — there still wasn't a free seat to be had — and the architect and Kirchner's pupil slipped in. All the customers clapped and cheered and raised their fists. Kirchner's pupil grinned as if they'd all pulled off an especially good trick, and the architect raised both hands in the air. They pushed their way through to the already over-full table and, both at the same time, and interrupting one another, said that, once the result was known, several bourgeois parliamentarians, even Federal Councillor Ebi, a Catholic Conservative and made of iron, had burst into tears. — As did, to the surprise of all present, Typesetter Wälti, when he realized he hadn't, in fact, been elected. My father, when that became clear to him too, began to beam again and ordered two more eaux-de-vie, one for himself and one for his unsuccessful comrade. The four Social Democrat candidates for the Federal Council had been confirmed straightaway, whereas the three Bourgeois ones hadn't secured a large enough majority and had to go into a second round of voting. That could have been a tacit election — three seats, three candidates, a simple majority, only, needed now — but, to the amazement of everyone, the architect — literally just elected to the town council, in glittering fashion — stood as a candidate. (My father hadn't known it was possible to come in only at the second stage.) And indeed: only a few hundred more votes for him, and it would have been all over for Herr Ebi. A communist would have replaced him as Director of Finance! — The 'List of Labour' then ended up with a representative on the Federal Council, after all. (Ebi was no longer crying. He threw a fit.) For the Social Democrats, deeply disturbed by the success of the 'List of Labour', organized a proper party tribunal, at which fifty-six members were accused of forming a communist cell and doing the groundwork for the world revolution, or rather, the 'List of Labour'. Thirteen of them were, indeed, excluded from the party. The most prominent among them, just re-elected with one of the best results, had been the front man for Education and Public Transport. Without a second's hesitation he switched to the 'List of Labour'—the suspicion of the *Sozis* had been justified—so that my father, suddenly, in fact, did have a comrade at the highest level, if the reform of all schools was now to become a reality.—Of course, the 'List' didn't remain a list but was turned, another few weeks later, into a party, the 'Party of Labour', into which all the communists from earlier, and many new ones, were accepted. The architect became its president. My father, too, joined the party at its inaugural meeting—in a once-again-full Volkshaus—and when, weeks later, the Party of Labour went nationwide, he was there for that, too. He travelled with a whole troop of comrades to Berne. On the journey back, he drank, together with his comrades, Chianti from demijohns, and ate, like everyone else, salami and bread, of which there was suddenly more than enough. (The women had brought baskets, which they now unpacked.) That was so enjoyable, they all had one last drink together in the second-class buffet at the station. A large table full of men and women, beaming happily at one another. When, beneath a full moon, my father went up the slabbed path to his front door, and looked up to see the dark nursery window, he remembered it was the Penguin's, his child's, birthday. He was six. (It was Rüdiger's birthday too.

He was thirty-six.) My father stood one of his Rütis outside the nursery door, and put in its hand an orchid he pinched from a vase in the 'warmth'. Clara liked orchids, and there always was one on the tiny little table in the corner. He was sure she wouldn't notice he'd violated the flowers. — In Rüti's other hand he placed a sign he cut out from the lid of a hundred-pack of Parisiennes; on it, he wrote 'Happy Birthday' though his son couldn't read yet.

ONLY INDIRECTLY did my father handing out Russian children's books at school, have anything to do with all that. Picture books, with short texts in Cyrillic letters. He'd got to know them, of course, through his communist friends. Kirchner's pupil was a passionate collector, and owned every illustrated book, just about, that had appeared in the Soviet Union since 1917. My father gave his pupils these colourful fairy tales because the text was incomprehensible. (He didn't know, either, what the stories were.) The pupils had to each invent a story in response to the pictures; and to write it in French. — That same evening, my father received an agitated call from the school secretary: the next morning, first thing, oh-seven-hundred, he'd to come and see the Principal. The Principal was raging. — The schoolhouse was modelled on the Palazzo Pitti in Florence, exhibitionist Renaissance, with broad staircases that my father climbed, just before seven. The schoolhouse was empty. He echoed his way along long corridors, and knocked on the door of the Principal's office. The school secretary, a grey little man, opened the door to him, and he entered. A gloomy big room, at the other end of which the Principal sat on the edge of his desk, on half a buttock and, therefore, crookedly; with one leg stretched out, straight as a

poker, as he was small and could reach the floor only with difficulty. He was wearing the uniform of a major in the trans-
mission troops, and black boots. The major's hat—with its
thick golden vermicelli—lay on the table beside him. In his
right hand he held an ink-smeared ruler; with it, he was hitting his left. His moustache that, a few weeks earlier, he'd
trimmed to look like Hitler's, now slanted at both ends. His
eyes, glassy, were popping out of their sockets. 'Communist
propaganda!' he shouted, holding up a book. 'At *my* school!'
My father went over to him—the secretary scuttled along
beside him—and took the book. It was from Kirchner's pupil's
collection. It was about a carrot, a gigantic carrot, that a
farmer couldn't get out of the ground, even when he pulled at
the leaves with all his might. So he called to his wife for help,
and she began to pull at the farmer who was pulling at the
carrot. The carrot didn't budge. A little girl happened to pass;
she pulled at the farmer's wife who was pulling at the farmer
who was pulling at the carrot. A boy with blue trousers, the
milkman, a dog, all followed. Only when a little birdie pulled
at the tail of the dog who was pulling at the milkman, at the
boy with the blue trousers, at the little girl, at the farmer's
wife, at the farmer, did the carrot give up and come shooting
out of the ground so suddenly that all the helpers tumbled
over one another, the farmer over the farmer's wife over the
little girl over the boy with the blue trousers over the milkman over the dog. The bird was alone in flapping its jubilant
wings over all of those who, in the final picture, were on their
backs with their legs in the air, laughing, because tonight
they'd a gigantic carrot to eat for dinner and because they'd
helped one another so kindly. 'Aren't you aware, Sir,' the Principal barked, 'that all forms of political propaganda are forbidden in our democratic schools?' My father said that political

propaganda, and communist, to boot, couldn't have been further from his mind, and that he'd simply wanted to stimulate the pupils' narrative imagination. 'Using Marxist-Leninist literature!' the Principal shouted, slipping from the edge of the desk, involuntarily perhaps, as he was now standing with both feet on the ground and having to raise his chin to look up at my father. (My father was no giant, either.) He took a piece of paper with several stamps on it from his desk and waved it, as he'd done with the book previously, at my father's face. 'I have a message here from the cantonal tax authorities,' he said, whispering almost, and stepping very close to my father. 'In all the years you have been at this school, so: eight, you have submitted not a single tax declaration to the cantonal tax people nor ever paid a single franc in tax.' His eyes grew even bigger, even glassier, and he barked again, his mouth close to my father's Adam's apple. 'I am going to start disciplinary proceedings against you,' he roared. 'I'll see to it that you never ever spray your red poison at an educational establishment in this country again. Dismiss!' — That evening, my father and Clara argued about money. About their joint money, for they'd a joint kitty — Clara, out of love, had absolutely wanted it that way; and my father couldn't imagine anything else — to cover everything, that included my father's salary — five hundred and sixty francs per month — and Clara's inheritance. One or two hundred thousand francs, every rappen of which she knew about, and so she also knew how much my father spent every month over and above his actual income. Records, books, rarely fewer than two or three a day. His French cut-flush bindings — volumes in the *nrf* series, for instance — he had bound in half-leather by Herr Schroth, with the result that his walls of bookshelves with books from France looked as if he owned many hundreds of copies of the *one* book. — My father had said nothing about the incident with the Principal, of course not. Clara raised the subject herself. (She'd a good nose for the right moment, and had been at the bank that morning.) She'd waited until the child was asleep—it should never have the feeling its parents were arguing—and so my father was already in the 'warmth', and in the process of taking his trousers off. 'Karl,' she whispered, closing the door quietly. 'This month again you've spent twice as much as you earn.' My father took his underpants off. 'Books!' She continued to whisper, more loudly. 'When do you *read* the books?' My father put his pyjama trousers on. 'Your records! You buy more records than you can possibly listen to!' My father took his shirt off. He pressed his lips together, and the veins on his temples swelled up. 'You give me a travelling manicure set as a present,' Clara said so loudly that, mid-sentence, she put both hands over her mouth. 'I can't find pleasure in a travelling manicure set'—her voice sounded choked now—'if it costs two hundred francs and I never travel.' My father, long since red in the face, put on his pyjama jacket, closed the buttons, the first, the second, the one at the bottom, then raised his head—'Say something, Karl,' Clara pleaded, shouted—and roared: 'Money! You and your money! Do *I* ever worry about money?' He tore the door open, at which the child had been crouching, pressing its ears—that it covered with both hands—against the panel. When the door opened so unexpectedly, it rolled into the 'warmth', at the feet of its father, who stormed over it, out into the corridor. 'In a democracy, it's a punishable offence, in any case,' he roared, when he reached the door of the apartment, 'for the management of a school to collaborate with the tax authorities.' He slammed the door behind him. 'Tax authorities?' Clara screeched, lifting her child. 'Where do the tax authorities come into this?'—My father struck out through the door to the garden that, for years afterwards, was off its hinges. It was dark. No moon, no stars. A fog, almost the height of my father, was creeping across the fields and so he was tripping, blindly, over clods of earth and roots and stones. Looking down he couldn't see his pyjama jacket, never mind his feet. His head, alone, was floating—as if someone had chopped it off—on this sea of ground-clouds. He snorted up and down for a while. This way, then that. A night bird cried, far off in the forest. A just-as-distant dog barked. At one point, he fell, and his head was in the fog, too. Before his eyes: a world of milk, until he managed up again. He was freezing—he'd only his pyjamas on, after all—and went back into the house. Clara was with the child in the nursery, trying to calm it. The door was half open. 'Why is Papa angry?' My father went back to the 'warmth', crawled beneath the blanket, and when Clara came to bed, too, half an hour later, he was asleep, or almost. He felt her putting a hand on his shoulder, and heard her murmur, 'What do you want? It exists, —money. It's not as if it's my fault either.' Her voice was barely more than a breath. He grunted and rolled onto his other side. Clara, as he could also hear, was trying to sleep, too. — The disciplinary process, a month later, proved unsuccessful. A panel consisting of a physics and a geography teacher in the school—two men the Principal could rely on—and of a representative of the Education Department, it is true, did conclude that my father represented a threat to public order; and, as regards his tax misdemeanours, that he'd acted with intent to defraud. And that he should be removed from teaching with immediate effect. But the Federal Councillor responsible for the trams and education, and therefore also my father, summoned him in as soon as he'd read the damning report. (They were both members of the same party, meanwhile.) He, too, was sitting on one buttock, on his desk— he was bigger than the Principal, though —and handed my father the indictment. 'Comrade,' he said and sighed. 'If by six o' clock this evening you haven't paid your tax debts, plus the interest payable on your arrears, and the fine, then not even I will be able to help you.' My father opened the briefcase he'd taken along, a shapeless leather monster, in which there was enough space, alongside all his teaching materials, for his Sachs-Vilatte dictionary and his interval snack. (My father especially liked the sugared spirals they sold at the Jacob bakery.) 'The school reform,' he said. 'We need, finally, to get going on the school reform. It's an electoral promise you made. Here it is. All worked out for you.' He took out a Leitz file, full of papers. By now, the Federal Councillor was sitting on his seat and playing with a model tram on the surface of the table. 'School reform?' he said, staring at the file. 'Who mentioned school reform?' My father— bewildered—looked from the folder to the tram in the Federal Councillor's hand and back again; then said, 'I did!'; then turned on his heel and left. It's possible he slammed this door, too, behind him. At home, in any case, he reached, without out a moment's hesitation, for the phone and called Tildi Schimmel, the only rich person who had come to mind on his way home. It wasn't her, but her husband, who lifted the receiver. Edwin Schimmel. 'I'll sell you my records,' my father said. 'Five or six thousand of them. Caruso. Busch, both Busch's, Slezak, Rachmaninov, everything. All of Toscanini. Louis Armstrong. "Ich wollt' ich wär' ein Huhn"'.—'How much?' Edwin Schimmel asked. My father quoted, down to the last rappen, the amount he owed the tax people. 'I have to have the money today.'—'That's fine,' Edwin Schimmel said, and put down the phone. My father sank into his chair. He put a hand on his heart, breathed in and out. He was sweating and freezing, simultaneously. He was still sitting there, like that, with a tightness in his chest, when the doorbell rang, and he opened the door to see Edwin Schimmel's chauffeur. (Beyond the garden gate was the Rolls.) My father accepted the banknotes, stuffed them into all his pockets, got on his bike and cycled into town. He reached the Tax Office just as a clerk was about to lock the door. 'You're in luck!' the boy said. — 'Aren't I just?' my father said. He paid his debt and got a receipt from the clerk, who didn't turn a hair. 'Enjoy the rest of your evening.' On the way home he bought roses for Clara, exactly eighty, a rose for each year of Clara's and his life. He asked, as he'd no cash on him, to be invoiced for them.

WHEN MY FATHER'S FATHER DIED, his son — my father — in keeping with the old custom, and received practice, had to fetch his coffin from his home village in order to bury him. The war was still on, but very far off by now. Trains were no longer running only for army purposes, and so my father — unlike on the occasion of his first visit — took the express train; then changed into a slow train, into one of those old carriages in which every compartment has its own door; and, finally, into a post bus, a yellow Saurer, that took him to the furthest end of a steep valley that became narrower and narrower, to a hamlet, surrounded on all sides by vertical rock-faces. The World's End, it was called. Enough space, just, for a driver to turn the bus. The few houses weren't actually the end of the world, however, for my father, on foot now, climbed one of the mountainsides, the eastern one, on a zigzagging path, and soon through a forest that smelt of mushrooms and where trunks of ancient pine trees lay on the ground, overgrown with moss. Once, very close, a deer sprang from its hiding place and, crying out, ran off. Woodpeckers were drumming at tree trunks; wild pigeons cooed; a cuckoo called. My father counted the calls: thirteen; a good omen. A stream, across which, again and again, narrow bridges led—little more than two tree trunks, placed next to one another—roared now on his right, now off down to his left. The path was so steep that my father kept stopping, to catch his breath and wipe his brow. He'd even thrown his just-lit cigarette into the stream, right after his first draw. Eventually, he stepped out of the forest—he'd reached the tree line; above him, snowless slopes; high up, narrow ridges—at the very spot where, thirty years before, on his initiation trek, emerging from the ravine in which the lightning had almost killed him, he'd hit the path and the stream. This path was wider now, and almost didn't climb any further. Butterflies were fluttering—those little ones you get in the mountains—and finches, flying, were swerving, boldly. A blue sky, the sun high. A mild wind. My father was now walking the familiar path; here, almost a road; and soon he reached the chalk rock formation that looked like the fingers of a gigantic hand. In front of him lay, as ever, the village, black wooden cubes with steep shingle roofs, and stables on wooden stilts with round stone bases. The gentle curve of the path followed the slope, the grass still grey, almost black. The first house, the blacksmith's, had no windows. A few dormers with tiny curtains, no more than that. At the door, a coffin; a single coffin. My father touched it and looked up the front of the building; but nothing moved, no one. So he continued. The village street still looked like a petrified wave of cobbles, it's true, but the puddles of donkey piss and the nettles had gone. The air, for my father, was a refreshment. When he reached the village square, the upper edge of the amphitheatre, the bell of the Black Chapel began to ring—a welcome?—and from the doors of all the houses stepped men and women, laughing and heading for the inn in front of which, as ever, were stacked the coffins. Some of the women were dancing, their men shrieking with delight and throwng their hats in the air, and they all moved so skilfully on the steeply descending cobbles that they arrived, in a jiffy, down at the inn, where, jostling happily, in the way my father had seen once before, they vanished. By the time, carefully putting one foot in front of the other, he, too, reached the inn, he'd again been alone for a while. A few soldiers, whose job was to lead the horses, were grooming them; and that was it. (With them, one or two mules, bumping their snouts against those of the steeds.) Above the door was a red—red!—metal sign with the words 'Salmen Bräu' on it. My father went through the gap in the coffins and entered the bar. It was empty—where had the men and women gone?—apart from an officer, a captain, who was sitting with his jacket unbuttoned at a table, and eating soup, a black roux soup, my father was familiar with it, he recognized the smell, and the officer was just pouring, as you do, half a glass of red wine into the dish. My father acknowledged him—a glance in reply—and sat down at a distant table, above which was a glass cabinet full of trophies, the cup prizes awarded, in the past, to the best coffins, and a Savings Club box. Now, he could hear the villagers again, his ancestors: they were making a racket in the adjoining hall. A lot of voices. Were these predecessors *always* celebrating, even on a workday, around noon?—My father lit a cigarette and watched as the officer used bread to clean his plate. Outside, the church bell was still ringing so violently that you could imagine both the pastor and the sexton hanging from the bell rope. In here, the bar area, wasn't any different from all those many years ago if my father ignored another red Salmen sign, lit from within, hanging over the counter. It was, indeed, the case: the inn—and with it, no doubt, the village—now had electricity. Round, white-glass lampshades on the ceiling; between them, a few flycatchers.—Finally, the door to the hall opened— the chattering and laughter was loud for a moment—and his uncle came in. He'd aged, of course, had white hair, and slouched as he walked. But it was his uncle, no doubt about it. The same eyes, the same mouth. He came over to the table.

'Yes?'

'I'm Karl,' my father said. 'Karl's son. He died yesterday.'

'So you've come,' my uncle said. 'Already.—What would you like to drink?'

'A beer.'

My uncle went to the counter, poured a beer and came back to the table.

'And you've come to fetch the coffin.'

My father nodded. His uncle put the beer down in front of him, and my father suddenly noticed how very thirsty he, in fact, was. He emptied the glass in a oner.

'We now sell Salmen beer,' his uncle said. 'We no longer brew our own.'

He went, heavily, across the bar to the entrance, opened the door and disappeared outside. He left the door open. Outside, the bright day was shining and the bell droned on. My father stood up—an accordion was now playing in the hall; the men and women were dancing, perhaps—and followed his uncle. The same one was standing before the mountain of wood and pointing to a coffin. 'That's it.' My father's father's coffin had, in the course of the years, slipped to the bottom row—beneath it, the earth, for which it was destined—and was covered in moss and mould. Above it lay a whole pile of younger coffins. My uncle gave it a kick — to check, not violent — nodded and called something over to the soldiers with the horses. 'It's that time again', or words to that effect. And two of the lads came right away, each with a big grin and, like they'd done this many times before, lifted the pile above my father's father's coffin and held it there while my uncle, niftily, pulled out the very bottom coffin. Then, not a moment too soon, the soldiers let their load drop. The coffins clattered down, and the whole mountain range trembled. A black wooden coffin with carved runes now lay at the bottom. 'Elianor,' his uncle said when he noticed my father looking. 'She went to America. That one there,' — he pointed with his chin to the neighbouring pile — 'is yours.' — My father stood the freed coffin on its end and put his back to it. He reached round with both hands and was about to lift his burden.

'Twenty rappen,' his uncle said.

My father let go of the coffin and looked at his uncle.

'The beer,' he said.

My father took a twenty-rappen piece from his wallet and gave it to him. 'While I see you,' he said, 'my maid of honour back then, the one with the freckles, how is she?'

'She still has freckles,' his uncle said.

'And apart from that?'

But his uncle was already on his way back to the inn. When he got to the door, he turned around and called, 'The war's over.'

'The war's over?'

'The war's over, and my brother has died.' He disappeared into the house. His feet apart to take the weight, my father got the coffin onto his back and set off, bending so low that he could only see the cobbles ahead of him. The war was over. That was why the bells were ringing! That's why the villagers where shrieking with joy in the hall! That's why the soldiers were in such a good mood! — The coffin was heavy, and, by the time my father got to the top of the square, he was drenched in sweat. He tapped his way blindly along the main street, seeing, at most, the thresholds of the houses. The coffins. At the blacksmith's, at the end of the village, he raised his head, looked up, right up to the hatch on the top floor — black glass, with a blue flower behind it — but when the coffin began to slide down his back he quickly leant forward again. There wasn't a sound from the house. So, with his eyes at ground level, like an animal, he continued on his way, his way back, past the Four-Finger-Rock, and, immediately after that, a chapel he'd never noticed, of which, now, he was only able to see the foundations, and in which — he could only see up as far as his chest — one of those gnome-like saints seemed to be standing that he could remember from his own ceremony in the Black Chapel. 'Help me, Man of God,' he said to him; a prayer; perhaps he would help. — The path through the forest was steep, so steep, my father went down it with big leaps. Voluntarily, or not. Shrieking with delight, groaning. The coffin knocking against his back. At one point, mid-jump, he spotted a sudden turn in the path so late that he landed on a slanting rock and, falling, had to cling to alpine rhododendrons. Somehow, he managed to get hold of the coffin, too, that was already bound for the ravine. — At the World's End, the bus was waiting. He put the coffin beside a container of milk on a rack at the rear, and sat down on the front seat. He was the only passenger. Chewing on a match, the driver steered the bus, negotiating, with majestic composure, his way along jutting rocks and bridge parapets beneath which raged wild waters. On a single occasion, before a *very* tight bend, he tooted the post-horn; perhaps he did this so rarely because it was so out of tune. — The slow train was also ready to depart. That said, the station master, a mere boy in a red cap, blocked my father's way when he wanted to get into one of the compartments. 'Passengers with bulky goods, such as travel chests or coffins, have to use the luggage van,' he said. And so my father had to stand, holding his bulky goods with both hands, as far as the station, where he changed into the express train. This time, he went straight to the luggage van. A railway employee helped him get the coffin onto the train. — He'd to get it off again himself. — From the station, he went home on foot. That wasn't much more than an hour; there'd been a crowd at the tram stop—it was the end of the working day—and he couldn't be bothered discussing the matter with the conductor. The sun was low on the horizon when he got to the house and, his eyes down at his feet still, went through the gate, up the path, and through the inner gate. He threw the coffin down on a carrot patch and, his body still at a right-angle, even without the load, dropped onto the lid. He landed so hard that the wood cracked, and he burst into tears. His heart was racing, his head pounding. After a while, nonetheless, through the roaring in his head, he heard something voice-like, loud, from above him, so he raised his head and really had to blink. On the first-floor terrace stood Rüdiger, between the two mastiffs that, like him, had their paws on the railing, and he was shouting: there he was, at last, my father; and that he'd had his fill, once and for all, of living beneath the same roof as a communist. Only respect for Clara had stopped him from saying so long before. Now, though, that the struggle against the brown variety of Fascism had been won, the battle against the red variety was beginning. He was giving him

notice: he'd to be out of the apartment by the first of the sixth.
'And there'll be no going back on that!'—Astor and Carino
were barking now too.—My father heard steps coming up behind him and tried to turn his head. Clara. Clara, in her blue
gardener's apron, and with pruning shears in her hand, sat
down beside him on the coffin—the wood of the lid creaked
again—and put an arm round him. 'Oh!' she sighed. He put
a hand on one of her thighs.—They sat there like that for a
while, staring ahead.—Throughout all this, two men had been
loading large piles of records onto the back end of a truck beyond the gate. Both were wearing blue overalls with the logo
of the local factory on their chests—a red M, with a crown
hovering over it—and were to-ing and fro-ing, fro-ing and to-
ing, their shadows becoming ever longer. At one point, one of
them dropped ten or even twenty records and, cursing to himself, kicked the remains into a ditch. Only when—in the last
light of the setting sun—they heaved the walnut Marconi onto
the loading surface, and closed the side panels, did my father
realize who they were and what they were doing. He went
over and gave them a tip.

(THAT NIGHT, my father was the first to read his father's white
book, though custom and tradition had it that the eldest son
should have that right. Only then was everyone else permitted to learn about the dead man's life. Felix, though he
respected rules more than his brother, wouldn't take it amiss.
—My father sat at his desk and read, page after page, day by
day, from 2 November 1885, his father's twelfth birthday, up
to the previous day. Outside, a wind was blowing, hitting the
cherry tree against the window. Clouds swept past the moon,
a half moon.—At one point, my father's head dropped onto

the book—he'd fallen asleep—and he got up, went into the
kitchen and drank a coffee. He then continued reading,
skipping not a single line. By the time he got to the last page,
day was breaking and the first birds could be heard. He read
as far as the last word, the final full stop. His father had perfect handwriting, the Sütterlin he'd been taught. It flowed,
calmly, from the first page of his book, to the last.)

MY FATHER, CLARA AND THE CHILD now lived at the other
end of town, in a suburb full of small houses with small gardens. Their house was even big, almost a villa, and cost so little rent—four hundred francs a month—only because it was
a wreck, with crooked window frames and walls from which
the plaster was falling; and because it belonged to Clara's—
after Hildegard—best friend. She was looking for someone
who would see to it that everything remained as her Papa,
who had died of influenza, in 1918, had known it; and as her
Mama had kept it. (She was a doctor, had never found a husband, and wished to be addressed as Fräulein—Fräulein Doktor.) She'd spent her childhood in this house and still used a
room on the ground floor, where she slept, sometimes, with
her dog called Nobs. She was now living in town, it's true, but
still came out to the suburb every evening in her pre-war Peu-
geot to check whether the nettles, as her father would have
wished, were still thriving between the steps of the outside
staircase; and that the porch above the front door was still a
rusty sieve. The plaster was grey, almost black; and mouldy.
(Fräulein Doktor, herself, looked a little like her house.)
When my father, the first time they visited the house—he was
enthusiastic, Clara felt humiliated—leant against the balustrade
of the balcony, a piece of masonry broke off and fell into the

garden. (It lay there, in the long grass, for many years.) Not
a single window closed properly. In winter, it snowed into the
rooms, though Clara sealed the gaps and cracks with strips of
felt. The floor, parquet flooring that had darkened in colour,
creaked so much that everyone always knew where everyone
else was. Anyone using the toilet and pulling the chain, always, just about, had to climb up on the seat to free the ball-
cock from the position it was stuck in, in the cistern—or the
water would've kept refilling. The heating—central heating,
yes, but one built around the turn of the century, for sure; a
prototype that had then been rejected, once and for all—de-
voured tons of coal but barely managed to get even just the
first floor halfway warm. My father was the boilerman. (In
later years, the grown-up child, me, took over this office.) At
five in the morning, or half past, he'd go down to the cellar,
open the front of the oven, take the shovel, go up two steps,
past suitcases and boxes to a slatted frame where the bikes
were parked, and turn once on his own axis—still holding the
shovel as a soldier would his lance—in order to enter, shovel-
first, a light-less tunnel, at the far end of which the coal was
concealed. He'd to bend as he went—the tunnel was, at best,
shoulder high; and so narrow that my father couldn't turn—
pushing the shovel ahead of him until he felt its resistance
under the coal. He jiggled and scraped till he thought the
shovel was full, then, walking backwards, felt his way back
to the bikes, straightened up, turned on his own axis again,
and went, upright now, and holding the full shovel level, to
one side, past the boxes and suitcases and down the two steps
to the heating. He tipped the coal in through the hatch. (If
he'd lost a few pieces of coal as he walked back, he'd stand
his shovel against the wall and go and collect them. Sometimes, too, he kicked them into a corner, just.) He would walk

this path a dozen times, until the oven was sufficiently full. — Normally, he let the heating die during the night. (Clara, who was never cold, insisted on it; she also calculated for my father what it would cost to keep on feeding this greedy fire-beast all night.) In the morning, he used a piece of apparatus, known as his 'sword', to light the coals; a metal pipe, originally — probably — a metre long, and closed at the tip, but with lots of small holes and fed with gas via a rubber tube. In the hands of a previous boilerman, perhaps even the Papa of Fräulein Doktor, it had broken in two and was now just a short stump, from which the burning gas raced as from a flame-thrower. When my father lit it, he never knew if he was about to blow up the whole house or set it alight. One or the other. Fortunately, he was a pyromaniac (in his youth, he'd burnt down the turnstyle of Old Boys FC though he'd only been aiming for the dry grass around it) and developed a way of lighting his 'sword' that I, the child, later didn't dare adopt. He wedged the pipe between his legs — the orifice, not too close to his privates — and struck a match with his right hand, shoved the matchbox into his pocket with his left, held the burning match at the still gas-less opening, and, with his now free left hand — in what was an acrobatic move — grabbed the gas switch on the wall his back was leaning against and turned it on. A flame shot out from between his thighs and flared across the room, to the wall opposite. The first time he did this, he, indeed, got such a fright, that he tried to save his legs — by parting them — and his 'sword', suddenly liberated, fell to the floor and, with flames flying from it, raced around the cellar like a dragon-snake gone mad. He turned off the gas and extinguished Clara's smalls that had been drying on a clothes horse. — But that didn't happen to him a second time. — He felt good in a house that Clara thought was terrible, and called

a ruin. 'A dilapidated hovel is what it is, a hole.' There was
more space for his books than in Rüdiger's Bauhaus aquarium.
The old, and a few new, bookshelves stood along all the walls
in all the rooms, and soon in the staircase, in both loos and in
the attic, too. — My father had a certain look, that flickered
between knowing and madness when he was looking for a
book. — He no longer had a gramophone, though. And not a
single record. After a few months, he bought a radio — 'Imagine — not a single rappen, did I have to pay as a deposit!' he
said to Clara — at the rear of which was mounted a little metal
box with a slit, into which — as with the gas metres once — he'd
to put a twenty-rappen piece to listen for half an hour. (The
seller came round once a month and emptied the box. He'd
count the coins, note the amount and give my father a receipt.
After six hundred thousand minutes of listening, the appliance
belonged to the buyer.) — Often, my father would sit, his ears
burning, in front of the radio, listening to a football match — he
could *see* it — and the machine would turn itself off when Hans
Hausmann (Radio Beromünster) or Squibbs (Sottens) was
in the middle of a sentence. Dead silence, though Hügi II had
just been passed the ball by Jacky Fatton. My father would
turn out all his pockets and crawl under the furniture, but, by
the time he'd finally found a twenty-rappen piece, Hügi II
had — long since — tripped over the ball again or the game was
over. — Eventually, there was a gramophone in the house again,
that white design-miracle produced by Braun, and my father
acquired the first record of his new collection. The LP had
been invented meanwhile (the first collector's item was
Beethoven's Piano Concerto No. 5, with Wilhelm Backhaus),
and, in the end, my father again had a thousand, or more, of
them. — Clara didn't mention records any more, and tuned off
if one was playing. But around the new house, too, there was

a garden, if a smaller one. It was big enough for a few pansies and lettuces, and the walnut tree — that almost filled it — was bigger than the one in Rüdiger's garden.

BENEATH THIS WALNUT TREE SAT MEN, each one different and yet all very similar. They'd arrive one after another, sometimes a few together, sit on the garden seats, crack nuts open and drink wine from Clara's uncle in the Piedmont who was now allowed to cross the border again. They were all young, all from Germany, and they all had a half-finished novel, or a few poems, in their leather bags. One was a publisher who — without a publishing company, without money and without books — was already drafting contracts for the works being discussed there in the garden. He, too, was gaunt, thin, smoked nervously, had a white face, untidy hair, un-ironed trousers and shoes with holes in them. He, like all of them, laughed a lot, their eyes serious. They'd survived the war (there wasn't a single woman in the group) and now everything was going to be different. — After two or three hours, they began to differ from one another. One spoke the dialect of the Rhineland, had a rounder face and was both a skeptic *and* a believer. One was from Berlin, said 'icke' instead of 'ich', and an incredible rage befell him whenever he thought of the invasion of Poland in which he'd been involved. One had been in Vyazma-Bryansk and lost three quarters of his lungs (a grenade that exploded). With the remaining quarter he spoke, sang and smoked more than all the others put together. One never spoke a word about the war. Ever. For him, only the future existed. One was small and quiet. One's leg had been shot to pieces; he didn't say much either. — They ate Clara's spaghetti, and my father's schnapps, the different kinds, were drunk even by those who had returned from the Caucasus or a prison camp with a damaged stomach. — My father now had a lot of contact with these writers, who had names like everyone and yet like no one, and who, for him, represented a new Germany. There *couldn't* have been only Nazis, and they were the proof of it. The hope in the future that was coming. He wrote long letters to Cologne, Berlin and Frankfurt, and sent his new friends kilos of coffee. (Throughout the entire war, he himself had always known where to get coffee. Even when not a single coffee bean had entered the country for a long time, legally, anyway, he went to a pharmacy near the main post office, made sure he was served by the boss, touched his nose with his thumb, mumbled, 'Three two-packs of Einmalzin for five shillings,' and would be given a readymade packet of coffee *and* the three two-packs.) — For some reason, it was strictly forbidden to send coffee to Germany — juicy fines, if you were caught — and so my father filled his gifts into large-format books he'd hollowed out with a book-binder's knife. *The Mountains of Our Homeland*, *Our Railway Stations*, *Volume 2* or *The National Exhibition of 1939*. Only the dust-jacket, the book's cover and the very first pages would remain intact. The sender was *always* Urs Usenbenz, Pilgerstrasse 7. That said, these illegal CARE packets smelled so strongly of coffee that it only rarely reached its destination unscathed. At times, the empty book arrived with the wrapping paper; often, nothing did. — My father had lost sight of the painters. They'd lost sight of themselves. It wasn't that the group no longer existed. On the contrary. It had more members than ever. After the war — the group had existed for twelve years by then, after all — a whole troop of young painters had been accepted into it. My father's friends, though, would sit more and more rarely with them at their table in the Ticino — presided over, meanwhile, uncontested, by Wälti, the failed parliamentarian—and my father was no longer the secretary. (Even those who liked him, and his work for them, agreed the kitty was better off in other hands.) The Surrealist now lived, for the most part, in Alsace, in a house overgrown with knotgrass, and looked, on those occasions when he did return to the distant town, like a wood gnome, one wearing a *béret basque*. He was painting more, and better, than ever, but only wanted to let people see his paintings when they'd the power of a landslide. He wasn't, he reckoned, quite there yet.—The lady painter painted bright views of towns and portraits, smoked, even in public, and let everyone see her love for her husband, still the only black man far and wide, who had set up as an ornamental blacksmith on the Münstersteig. He would stand there, a magician surrounded by spraying sparks, hammering away at a red-hot iron. In the evening, his wife would come and watch, admiringly, until he'd finished; then off they would walk, arm in arm.—The genius from the Weinland region lay buried beneath a weeping willow.—The wire sculptor now tolerated, alongside the wire, the plaster and his shade of yellow, a splash of red at times and a dash of ultramarine. He doubted himself a lot and would smash his formations before the plaster had set.—Shortly after the proclamation of the German Democratic Republic, the architect went to Berlin; there he was given a large office at the Academy and planned entire towns, models of a new form of communal living. He was given the Stalin Prize, got to shake hands with Wilhelm Pieck, but not one of his projects was actually built.—Kirchner's pupil painted aggressive paintings full of shining beauty, travelled once to Moscow, returned enchanted, and formed a society to promote friendship between Switzerland and the Soviet Union. He became its president. He remained, of course, a member of the Party of Labour, and of the town council, arguing that everyone should be equal before the law. At an improvised meeting—the last to take place in the room at the Ticino, all the later ones happened at the Casino—a majority of the painters decided to exclude him from the group he had helped found. Politically, he was no longer acceptable in their eyes; perhaps because the very people whom he attacked, untiringly, were their best customers; and, no doubt, also because they painted less well than he did. (The Surrealist had no idea about the planned putsch and stayed in Alsace. The architect was in Berlin. The wire sculptor, also caught on the hop, voted against the exclusion and left the meeting with the lady painter who was raging and crying.)—My father, of course, was no longer part of it. He thought this rebellion of small minds repulsive—he heard about it, more by chance, days later—but, nonetheless, didn't arrange to meet Kirchner's pupil ever again. It just didn't happen. (Once, he bumped into him at the Historical Museum. They spoke about this and that, and soon parted.) And when he then, once, had toothache, he didn't go to Kirchner's pupil's wife, as before—she was a dentist and her practice was near the zoo—but chose a Dr Meier, whom Myrta, a neighbour, had recommended to him and from whose treatment chair he could look into the offices of the merchant bank.—He didn't ever formally leave the party. He simply read *Vorwärts* less and less closely, and neglected to pay his subs. When there were votes, he only sometimes followed the party line now, and no longer always. And so he ceased to be a party member without really being sure about it.

MYRTA WAS THE WIFE OF AN INDUSTRIALIST—his name was Arnulf, Arnulf Kerz—who produced electrical items somewhere in the Swiss Midlands. Toasters, irons, coffee mills. She lived far up the mountain, where the forest began, with her husband, two daughters at the giggly stage and a maid who growled in Italian. Not far away, nonetheless. My father and Clara, on their first visit (Clara's last) climbed a steep road that took them, in less than ten minutes, to the house. It was a proper villa with Roman columns on either side of the door, rhododendron in the front garden, and, further back, a large tulip poplar. The road led past a park-like garden, though, full of firs and oaks, along the wooden fence of which two black dobermen raced, barking and baring their teeth. My father had had his fill of flesh-eating dogs, and so, on his second visit—without Clara this time, and the next day—made a detour that took a good half hour. Out and along to the re-formed church, then up the mountain, then back between the edge of the forest and the allotment gardens full of flags, and—finally—along Dobermen Street from the other end.—My father and Clara first visited Myrta and Arnulf, having been invited to one of their home concerts. A card, made of handmade paper, with a deckle edge and lettering reminiscent of someone's handwriting. RSVP. How my father and Clara came to be among the select few remained Myrta's secret. She smiled at my father when he asked, and said he'd a very beautiful wife.—The other guests were industrialists like Arnulf, and wives or neighbours. A woman who had married into the de Montmollin family, too. Edward de Montmollin, her husband, imported cigars and was on a business trip, in Havana, or Istanbul, perhaps.—The attraction of the evening was a pianist, and—as the group of guests, with whom my father and Clara drank a glass of white wine to get in the mood, and to whom Madame de Montmollin also belonged, assumed quite naturally—the lady of the house's lover. The lady in question was soon clapping her hands—she beamed at

each guest, individually, and pointed to the door of the salon —
and they all sat down on empire chairs, or kitchen stools with
pink cushions, that had been placed in a semicircle around a
grand piano. (Madame de Montmollin, although by no stretch
of the imagination old and venerable, was permitted to sit in
an armchair that had gold-painted feet.) — The pianist entered
the stage through the garden door. He was wearing tails, and
bowed in such a way that his hair fell over his face like a curtain. He played Beethoven's Diabelli Variations — Diabelli's
theme was what he played best — and after the first bars was
already soaked in sweat. Myrta watched his whirling fingers
with a steadfast gaze, and Arnulf looked at his wife with eyes
that shone: how she succeeded again and again in bonding
with splendid artists. (The previous artist — my father and
Clara hadn't been invited at that point — had been a singer, a
tenor, who had sung under the direction of Ansermet; and,
before him, had been another pianist, one who liked to play
music in historically correct fashion, for whom Arnulf had
hired, specially, a hammerclavier from when Haydn was
alive.) — The pianist bowed to quiet applause and immediately
gave an encore. Rachmaninov, or perhaps Tchaikovsky, a
Russian-sounding piece, in any case, in which he invested the
strength of all his fingers. In the meantime, the lady of the
house — something she hadn't done at the earlier concerts —
passed a plate round, on which she, to start things off, had
placed a twenty-franc note. This alienated her guests —
certainly the rich among them — so very much that they added
a note and then left; without saying goodbye, almost. Madame
de Montmollin even ignored Myrta, and offered only Arnulf
her hand, who — taken aback — did something like kiss it. A
few minutes later — the guests headed silently towards the
door, as if fleeing — only Myrta, Arnulf, the pianist, my father,

Clara and a neighbour — the only person not to have dressed
up, who was wearing a tartan shirt and leather boots — were
left. Myrta glossed over the scandal with a great deal of
charm — she'd humour in abundance — and Arnulf had no idea
why his guests had left so quickly. The pianist, standing beside
his piano, drank, at the speed of his encore piece, several
glasses of white wine. — The six who remained sat down again,
here and there — there was, after all, no shortage of seats —
putting the glasses and the bottles on the floor, in front of
them, or on the piano. Myrta sat next to my father. (Arnulf
was taking care of the pianist, and Clara was sitting with the
neighbour with the boots.) Myrta and my father spoke about
Céline and the fact he was a terrible Nazi — but what a book,
the *Voyage au bout de la nuit*!; about Paul Léautaud and his
eighty cats; about how, according to a survey, Johanna Spyri
was the favourite author of German girls, *German* girls,
whereas, in the case of the boys, Karl May was ahead of the
rest; but, mainly, their conversation focussed on the question
of whether or not Goethe had slept with Frau von Stein.
Myrta was of the opinion that he had, and justified this by
saying that a lady of the highest Weimar society had five
senses, too, and wouldn't be able to resist someone like
Goethe. Above all, if her own husband was so wooden. My
father believed that not so much Frau von Stein — she, in any
case, would have been — but Goethe himself had been too
inhibited to move beyond playing with burning words. Only
in Rome, when Father and Mother and therefore also Frau
von Stein had been at a sufficient distance, had he finally been
able to take the beautiful Faustina to his room, or rather she
him. 'He was about forty, in any case, at that point.' — 'And
Marianne von Willemer?' Myrta said. — 'Her, perhaps,' my
father said, laughing. 'In the shooting-box. On the wooden

table.' — The other guests were having great conversations, too. Arnulf told the pianist that his playing really made listeners feel happy, he could play faster than people could think. 'Than *you* can think,' Myrta called over, from where she was in a conversation with my father that she immediately resumed. Arnulf, who had German parents, and who spoke the dialect of the town's upper class especially carefully, told the pianist that that was right, his wife was more more intelligent than he. When he was right, though, he was right, and these Diabelli Variations had made him feel very happy. — Clara had learnt, meanwhile, that the neighbour with the colourful shirt and leather boots was the owner of the dobermen, and told him she'd had dogs before, too. The neighbour smiled and said they were such lovely animals, loyal, the only problem, really, was: they didn't like this particular dog, the dog in this house, a wire-haired dachshund with an impeccable pedigree, and had once almost ripped him to shreds after chasing him through the flowerbeds. — Myrta let out a big laugh, my father grinned and lit another cigarette. Clara looked over to them both, but she'd missed the punchline. — She and my father — and the neighbour, too — left well after midnight. My father was pretty tipsy, and, when he turned around again at the front door, Arnulf and Myrta were in the salon, and, between the two, the pianist was swaying to and fro. All three waved.

THE NEXT DAY, IN THE EARLY AFTERNOON, Myrta phoned and told my father, who had lifted the receiver, that last night had been a wonderful evening, thanks to him and his charming wife, new acquaintances who had enriched her life, and it had been wonderful for her to be able to speak from the heart about Goethe for once, again. In her everyday life, she was a bit short-changed in that respect. Did my father feel like dropping in for a cup of tea? 'Now, right away, in half an hour?' — My father said, 'Yes, gladly, of course' and left immediately as he wanted to take that detour. This time, the dachshund was wandering about the garden, and came running up when my father rang the bell, and barked a little. But *this* dog was feared by not even my father. — Arnulf was at the factory, the girls were at school, but the maid was there and brought them tea and cakes. (She'd the muscles of a weightlifter, and was called Delia.) The salon was no longer a concert hall, and Myrta and my father sat opposite one another on the empire chairs. This time they spoke — and, right away, with the same fiery passion — first about the book my father was currently translating, Julien Green's *Varouna*, and then, jumping from one idea to another, about the Cote d'Azur as a refuge for successful artists (Picasso, Somerset Maugham); about Arnold Zweig and how life in Palestine hadn't just been a picnic for him; about Anne Frank and her diary, and how a dozen German publishing houses hadn't wanted to publish it (my father knew the father in the family) until Lambert Schneider decided, after all, to do so; about Max Brod and how splendid it had been that he recognized, without being envious, that his friend Franz wrote much better than he himself did; about Stefan George, whom my father couldn't stand, and whom Myrta — though she also regarded him as an incense-dauber — her coinage, making them both laugh a lot — found impressive. My father didn't like Rilke either; and mocked his countesses and the white elephant that turned up every now and then; and Myrta quoted, to prove to my father how good Rilke, in fact, was, the poem about the gracious swans that dip their heads in the sobering holy water. She realized, just in time, Hölderlin had written it. Now, both were laughing even more. — When my father, at sundown, took the detour in the opposite direction — Dobermen Street, edge of the forest and allotments, down the slope and back from the church — he was glowing with enthusiasm and, once home, immediately prepared a pile of books he wanted to take along to Myrta next time. Of course, there was a next time, and a third and fourth time. They now also talked about music; about Schubert and what a poor so-and-so he'd been with women; about Mozart and why good society had dropped him: not because of his gambling debts but because the *Figaro*, that cheeky call for revolution, *couldn't* possibly please a Viennese nobility that was behind the times. Never mind the Kaiser. (Myrta was of the opinion something much more serious must have happened. Mozart had put his hand up the skirts of the Empress, or given her behind a little slap, or something.) — When my father visited for the fifth or sixth time, Delia wasn't there either, and Myrta and soon he, too, were blabbing less than on previous occasions. This time, they were sitting next to one another on the divan, looking into one another's eyes, drinking one sip of tea, then another. The birds were making a racket. Finally, Myrta touched one of my father's hands, by chance, or perhaps she simply took it, and they fell towards one another and began kissing. My father took his glasses off. His cigarette was in the hand that had reached for Myrta's head. His other hand was stroking her back. Their lips burrowed into one another's, they bit one another. Myrta's dress slipped up, or was pulled up, my father had no trousers on any more, and they were rolling and turning on the divan, and gasping and moaning and rejoicing, and, when they came back down, Myrta over my father, they were no longer on the divan but lying on the rug. Myrta's smalls were hanging like a flag from her right foot. The cigarette was playing with fire on the rug. Baschi, the wire-haired dachshund, was over by the window, panting. — My father took his leave soon afterwards — Myrta kissed him passionately — and took the detour back. He'd a sleepless night, tossing and turning, turning the light on and off — in the new house, in the old villa, he and Clara slept in separate rooms — he leafed through this book or that, ate an apple and drank some water but still couldn't get to sleep. — The next day, he visited Myrta again. He turned up without telling her, immediately after lunch, as he knew Myrta slept until very late in the morning. This time, the giggling teenagers and Delia were there. The girls ran through the salon at times, on their way from their rooms to the garden, and back again, and Delia was bustling around in the corridor. (Arnulf, at least, was at the office.) My father told Myrta it had been wonderful yesterday, overpowering, it had made a different person of him; or, to put it better: had helped the other person within him to see the light of the world. But this love was impossible. He couldn't do it. 'I love Clara, It's impossible.' Myrta was looking ahead, looked him in the eyes, and looked ahead again — the girls thundered past in the background — and whispered she understood; she, after all, loved Arnulf too; had he been disappointed by her; just as she'd been; a bit surprised, perhaps, by his stormy manner. She hadn't expected that at all.

'No!' my father exclaimed. 'But Clara!'

'And Edwin Schimmel?' Myrta whispered, putting a finger up to his lips. 'Did he never bother you?'

'Edwin Schimmel? What's Edwin Schimmel got to do with it?'

'*You* are asking that?' Myrta whispered, even more gently. 'Clara used to eat from the palm of his hand, everyone knew that. You know that, too.'

'Know what?'

'Well, that suddenly he was marrying this Tildi person, and, with her, the entire firm; and not even four weeks later, Clara married the first man to come along. I mean, everyone was saying that, you know what people are like—the way they talk.'

My father jumped up, stormed across to the door and ran down the steep street, past the dobermen raging alongside him, and on the verge of leaping over the hedge, not that he even realized.—Clara was in the garden, in her blue apron, with a watering can in her hand and speaking to her helper in the garden, a leathery man; my father never knew: was his name Herr Kern or Herr Wagner? A retired border guard, in any case, who carried out all his jobs at the double. Now, too, as he was speaking to Clara—so loudly, my father could hear every word: it was to do with using nettle juice to kill the snails, or to chase them away—the same one was loading, as if walking on hot coals, a wheelbarrow with torn-out weeds, he then rushed off with it, still speaking, disappeared—really screaming now—behind a bush, and was back before the end of his sentence with an empty barrow. 'We're not exactly short of nettles, after all.'—Clara spotted my father and waved to him. My father waved back and went into the house.—For a few weeks, he didn't see Myrta again. But he thought of her, of how she'd flung her legs in the air, how she laughed, of her eyes. His heart missed a beat each time he saw a woman turn a corner in the distance, or vanish into a shop.—Then he did, in fact, meet her. She came out of a hairdressing salon, her hair bright blonde and up in a stack, threw her arms round him, and the first thing she said was: she'd met an amazing artist—'Imagine, he's a bongo player'—and was on her way to him, he wanted to play his bongos for her. 'Will you walk with me a little?' My father walked with her. They spoke about the rich rhythm traditions of other cultures, and, outside a grey, rented house, Myrta stopped, gave my father a kiss on the cheek and said, 'It won't take more than an hour. Come and get me.' She disappeared into the house. My father went to the bookshop at the square outside the church and flicked through Alpine calendars and travel guides. An hour later, he was outside the house again. Hardly ten minutes later, Myrta came out. Her hair was now down, and she hooked her arm in his. She walked alongside him, triumphant and radiant.

'*PAIN*,' my father wrote in his white book, late in the evening of 3 April 1954 (it was his fifty-first birthday, and he and Clara had celebrated in the Red Ox, a restaurant on Rebgasse). '*I've always had pains. Ever since I was no longer a child, such that I've forgotten what it would be like to live without pain. I wake every morning with my head hammering,* every *morning! and am afraid of my skull exploding. 4 a.m., five, it's hardly ever later. — My heart feels tight, irregular. Racing heartbeat, often no heartbeat for moments of profound terror. Stabbing pains. My chest feeling encircled. Heartbeats, as if they were my last. This certainty of dying, this sure feeling! (Breaking into sweats: but sweating doesn't hurt. Like the stupid fact: what help is my large brain?) My heart feeling as if it might explode. The heart muscles, as if they'll hold this one last time. The arteries, as if they were being torn right now. The signals up to the brain raising almost every time the final alarm. And then I live, nonetheless, for a few minutes more. No little arteries tearing, no bursting vessels yet, despite everything: no sudden collapsing, though my temples are hammering, and stars are dancing across my retina. — I clench my teeth so much my jaws hurt. The chin, a hardened bundle of muscle, and often a shooting pain across the left (not ever, to date, across the right) cheek and up to my ear. — Neuralgias. The trigeminus, if that happens,* this *pain drives you mad. — The nerves tremble, all of them, always. Everything trembles, except perhaps on the surface. The outer skin: not it, not always. But the lips! How much more all the internal organs, joint trembling involving the spleen, the gall bladder, the liver and the kidneys. The eyelids flutter. — In my hands, ants — that suddenly wake up and, without reason, go to sleep again. (When in pain, I lose any sense of humour.) — A ring round my skull too, a smaller one than the one round my chest. At the periphery of my vision: shadows, fog, black plumes. As if I were wearing a lead cap. Blinkers. Am I a horse? — (When I'm in pain, even jokes hurt.) — Tears. Pains press the water out. No one has ever seen me cry, ever, I'm sure of it. Clara hasn't; and Fuzzy Bear, definitely not. He's a child, sixteen. (Last Christmas, when everyone was happy, when I was happy, tears suddenly shot from my skull. I held my hands over my eyes and laughed with my mouth.) — The small of my back hurts. (Pain is a silent cry.) The muscle's scream travels up to the back of my neck. — Between my legs, a pin; as if I were sitting, walking, on a nail. The nail-pin is in me, sharp, hurting, even if Dr Grien says there's no organ there. 'Only tissue. Nothing.' That nothing can make you raving mad, I am the proof. — Yes. — The kidneys. My skin is so yellow that, in the morning, in the mirror, I see an eighty-year-old Chinese man. (In front of the mirror, in the morning, humour abandons me.) Dr Grien says too, either give up the Treupel, or it's all over for the kidneys. (Treupel, a painkiller, contains Phenacetin. Phenacetin and nothing else on earth* [except, probably, morphine] *sorts out the migraine, and it destroys, gradually, but all the same, your nerves.) — The doctors?* Browny told me when I was thirty-one or perhaps thirty-three — l'âge du Christ — *I'd only three months to live. My heart, and if I continue to smoke like that. I'm still alive, and I'm still smoking.* Without *cigarettes, I'd be dead. So, I'm counting on my kidneys holding out a bit longer.* Et puis merde. *Sometimes, in the fire of the moment, in my enthusiasm about a well-written sentence, or in love, in those mad seconds of ecstasy, the pain goes away. (I love too little. But how. But when. But whom.) Only afterwards, when pain is torturing me again, do I realize: it was gone. I hadn't been feeling it! A pain you don't feel isn't one. Magnificent moments that fly off as I become certain of them, because, with thinking, pain returns. —Does pain ever sleep? At night, when exhaustion has become greater than it, and I've fallen asleep, I don't dream about it. About fear, about terror, that I do; but never about pain. In my dreams, the soul hurts, not my body. —The medication is in the drawer of the bedside table. Unlocked. It's so full, the little jars and tubes spill out when I open it. Pills, drops, syrups, I never throw anything away; here lie my medicines since 1933. Like the rockstrata of a mountain, of a 4,000-metre mountain; or like the rings of an old oak. At the very top, the medicines I need, so the Treupel, the Luminal, the Pervitin. —The old packets and little bottles conceal the revolver. It's at the very bottom. The temptation to shoot the pain to bits is great. With one blow, to kill pain off. Behind the pain shines something bright, light. —Should I not move ever again, become motionless, com-pletely motionless, or should I run, roaring, into my foe, my murderer, who will release me with a crushing blow of his halbert? —Celebrated my birthday in the evening. With Clara in the Red Ox. Phil Heymans is the manageress there —she hasn't been singing for years —but she wasn't there. I asked about her. She'd a stroke two months ago and is paralyzed down one side. But it's improving. —Small quarrel with Clara, because lobster was on special offer, and so I'd ordered a lobster, but then the advertised price turned out to be for 100 grammes, and not the whole lobster. Cost three hundred and forty francs, and not eight.'*

AT SOME POINT OR OTHER in the course of those years, my father was outside the house —waiting for the postman — when a car, far off still, turned into the road and began to draw closer, a lime-green convertible. Braking with style, it stopped in front of my father, and from its brown leather seats emerged a brown-from-the-sun man in a similarly green suit, and the same boy was one of the nameless men who, soon after the war, used to sit under the walnut tree. Now, he had a name, Joseph Caspar Witsch, the publisher without a publishing house, back then, who now had a publishing house. He and my father hugged, and, as Jupp Witsch made for the familiar walnut tree, taking those huge big steps of his, my father realized, gasping, behind him, that the times in which *he*'d been able to be generous and good, were gone. Sitting with his legs crossed—immaculate folds in his trousers—in the most comfortable chair, Witsch spelt out his plans: what he planned, generally; and what he planned, in particular, with my father. He'd everything ready: titles, deadlines, flat-rate fees. The amounts involved were substantially smaller than once imagined beneath the walnut tree, but my father, instantly enthusiastic, agreed to everything right away; signed the contracts, without a moment's hesitation; and, without stopping for breath, listed another dozen projects Witsch immediately found enlightening and important, and for which—verbally, initially—he also drew up contracts.—While Witsch poured himself a beer, my father went into the bathroom and swallowed an extra Treupel.—At that time, he was tackling so much that he began something new almost *every* day. A book. A series of books, a series of articles, a book review, an afterword: until the pains, as every day, got out of hand, and he gave up for *today*. (He was still also working at the school, of course. For a few years, he'd a reduced teaching load, and at the end of the decade he was declared to be an *invalid* and freed from teaching.)—He would work—even if the pains won their daily battle in the early evening—ten or even fourteen hours a day: he hardly ate any more, had to keep to a diet that strictly forbade salt (the kidneys), and wasn't permitted any more than 30 grammes of egg-white per day; that is, as much as is present in two slices of bread. Clara would cook, using their letter scales. —That didn't prevent him from translating pretty much everything written by the author he loved most passionately alongside and after Diderot, that is, Stendhal, whose real name was Marie-Henri Beyle, and whose works (dedicated *'to the happy few'*,) my father tackled one after the other: *Le Rouge et Le Noir*, *La Chartreuse de Parme*, *De l'Amour*, *Armance*, *Lamiel*, *Vie de Henri Brûlard*, *Lucien Leuwen*. But, of course, he also translated, in-between and alongside these, other books by other authors —his translations soon filled a cupboard; he gave them all as gifts to Clara, and she didn't read them —for example, *Mon oncle Benjamin* and *Belle-Plante et Cornélius* (Tillier), *Manon Lescaut* (Abbé Prévost), *Madame Bovary* and *L'éducation sentimentale* (Flaubert), *La cousine Bette*, *Contes drôlatiques*, *Peau de chagrin* and *Gobseck* (Balzac), *Mademoiselle Fifi*, *Boule de suif* or *Le horla* (Maupassant), *Nana* (Zola), *Poil de carotte* (Renard), *Patapoufs et Filifers* (Maurois), *Les liaisons dangereuses* (Choderlos de Laclos), *Le grand testament* (Villon) —the ballads, too —*La jument verte* and *Les tiroirs de l'inconnu* (Aymé), *Au bon beurre* (Dutourd), *Le bourgeois gentilhomme*, *Le malade imaginaire*, *Les précieuses ridicules* and *L'avare* (Molière), *Candide* and *L'ingénu* (Voltaire), *Carmen* (Mérimée), *Le poète assassiné* (Apollinaire) or *Gargantua et Pantagruel* (Rabelais). And many more. For instance, Mark Twain's *A Connecticut Yankee in King Arthur's Court*, though he'd not learnt English at school and never been to Britain. Or America. ('I learnt my English at the cinema,' he'd say.) —And the nuns and monks were honoured again, for he translated, for Witsch, sixty old French farces and novellas, in which the heroes from earlier in his life once again got stuck in: eating, drinking and knowing one another. — Diderot was the only one he didn't translate; almost not at all. A few short plays, and he wrote an afterword to Goethe's German version of *Neveu de Rameau*. He swallowed a pill every two or three pages. A hundred or three hundred per book. Every day, he wrote his sentences, and, day after day, the pain, finally, swept him from his chair. — Immediately after the war, as soon as it was at all possible, he travelled to Germany; to Stuttgart, first of all. It was shortly before Christmas, and the train that did the entire journey at a crawl was so full that the passengers (eight or ten per compartment, the children on the luggage racks) were standing in two lines in the corridor. Behind my father, at the window with his leather briefcase tucked under his arm, stood a man whose luggage was a Christmas tree. The branches were jabbing the back of my father's knees, such that he'd his knees bent throughout the entire journey, and was like the walking wounded when he arrived at Stuttgart Station; no one noticed; one in every two there was walking crooked. — Bad pains were shaking others, too. In that respect, he was also in good company. — It was Gerd Hatje that took him to Stuttgart, a young publisher with bold plans, and in his brief-case he carried his concept for a 'Janus Library of World Lit-erature', a series of books that would be co-produced by three publishing houses in Germany, Austria and Switzerland (and then, actually, was): by the aforementioned Gerd Hatje, as well as Willy Verkauf in Vienna and, finally, Arthur Niggli in Teufen. — Hatje and my father immediately came to a great understanding and spoke about books (my father) and pic-tures (Hatje) no one else knew. Once, they went to a cafe on Königstrasse that, like all the buildings on this former boule-vard, was makeshift and single-storey, and they ate gateau with cream which my father thought was dreadful. Inedible. Outside the window at which they were sitting, men and women — not just children — were jostling and staring at their plates. — They also went — Gerd Hatje had film-star looks and knew about fashion — to a factory that produced materials, to be more precise: *a* material, a rough, brownish-grey woollen material, this, and only this material, with the result that the janitor and the secretaries and the apprentices and the director all wore it. A dull colour, not a colour at all, actually; but it excited my father — deeply familiar, as it was, to him from distant ancient times — such that he bought a few metres. Gerd Hatje did so, too, with the consequence that, when he and Clara set off a few months later — Gerd was a frequent guest of my father's by then — on a joint trip to Italy, unexpectedly, from one day to the next, so to speak, both were dressed in the same cloth. Tone on tone. My father stood, waving, outside the house and could no longer tell the difference between them by the time they reached the end of the road. The indicator of Gerd's new car, a Borgward, flashed, and they were off. They remained missing for two weeks — furnishing Gerd's holiday home, south of Naples — and returned, beaming with happiness, Clara in an almost see-through dress with lots of red flowers, and Gerd in white trousers and a blue sports jacket. It was just the captain's hat that was missing. (Willy Verkauf, with whom my father and Clara, of course, also soon became acquainted, was so charming — he was Jewish *and* the heir to the very best of the k.u.k monarchy manners — that Clara thought he was a fraud; wrongly; later, he began to paint and had a career that went way beyond that of the publisher. — Arthur Niggli was from Thurgovia.) A Herr Rosenstein *was* then a cheat. He drove up in an open MG, was wearing driving gloves (the palms made of leather, the back of

the hands a mesh of fine threads) and had founded a publishing house that had, until now, published only *one* book (*The
way we talk*, *just*, a bit of a bestseller in the town) and who, if
you could believe him—as my father did but not Clara—
wished to devote the rest of his life to my father's creations.
For that, he needed an advance, all the same—he was very
young and an orphan—ten or twenty thousand francs, not a
lot if my father compared the sum to the blossoming publishing house and its profits. My father gave him the money,
behind Clara's back, and Clara sobbed tearlessly, and
punched away at my father with her little fists, when she discovered the hole in the kitty and learnt that Herr Rosenstein,
a few weeks before, had disappeared without trace. My
father roared, 'What can *I* do about it if Rosenstein's a pig?',
slammed the door shut behind him, and stomped up and down
the garden.—He then sat on the stump of a chopped-down
cherry tree and struggled for breath. His heart was racing,
missed a beat, then galloped off again. He went into the house
and swallowed a handful of pills but to no effect.—A few
years later, at the pharmacy (where he'd once bought coffee)
he suddenly found himself next to Herr Rosenstein who was
trying, without a prescription, to get medication for which a
prescription is needed. Both pretended not to recognize the
other.—My father quarrelled badly with Witsch a dozen times
and, on eleven occasions, became reconciled with him again.
Fortunately, a few days after the twelfth time, he got to know
Fräulein Winkler and Herr Dickschat, a couple that wasn't a
couple, and that ran a publishing house in Munich. Fräulein
Winkler was a delicate lady and responsible for their cata-
logue—classics, *all* the classics— and Herr Dickschat was her
reality man. He knew the figures, the percentages, calculated
the chances and the risks. He'd only one arm. He also *drank*.—

Fräulein Winkler and Herr Dickschat were to be my father's last great love, a passion marked by beautifully made books: India paper, lead typesetting, gilt edging, ribbon, stitched binding. Every edition cloth- or leather-bound. — With Herr Dickschat, my father negotiated the first contract that promised him, instead of a flat-rate fee, a percentage of the sales. Two per cent! Ancillary rights! One of my father's favourite activities — he was someone, normally, who never did his sums — was to work out the hourly rate of a translator. Thirty rappen, he made it, on days on which he was in especially good form; twenty-five otherwise. — Fräulein Winkler had a single editor — the firm was *very* small, Fräulein Winkler's salon and Herr Dickschat's den — whose name was Tanner, Herr Tanner, and who spoke such strong Lower Bavarian that my father didn't understand him. Ever. Hardly ever. They'd walk up and down, debating, nonetheless, Herr Tanner arguing with great seriousness, and my father with his sudden rages, whereby he didn't even know whether he was right, or wrong, to have them. — He was offended, in any case, when checking the proofs of any new translation, by every comma that had been inserted, and wrote letters to Herr Tanner that were pages long, in the assumption that the latter could at least *read* Standard German. (Herr Tanner, apart from Standard German, could speak French, Italian, Spanish and English. That said, when it came to actually *speaking* — to quoting Hölderlin, Voltaire, Petrarca, Lorca or Shakespeare — it sounded as if *all* of these writers were from Vilshofen.) — A few of the other men who had sat beneath the walnut tree had made a name for themselves now, too. They were now called Nonnenmann, Schnurre, Böll. With them, and soon with many others, my father organized readings, in the assembly hall of his school, that, more and more, was becoming his former school. It began with his friends, but the likes of Wolfgang Hildesheimer, Hans Bender and Günter Grass soon came too, as did, eventually, a very young Hans Magnus Enzensberger, who hopped around at the blackboard like a flibbertigibbet, explaining to the audience, who — the pupils excepted — were twice his age, how he wrote poems.

THE EVENING BEFORE HE DIED, my father had arranged a reading — the fiftieth, or perhaps the eightieth, in a now long series — with a lyric poet who had become something like the country's *doyenne* and who *never* did public appearances. Not ever. She'd become a legend, both famous and invisible. She lived in the mountains somewhere, in a remote place, in any case. Photographs of her didn't exist as she refused to have anything to do with photographers, and would vanish behind a barn if one was lying in wait on the village street. — And so my father had never dared to invite her to read, hadn't even considered the possibility, and then he did dare. Wrote her a letter, c/o her publisher. She replied by return, pleased, finally to be invited by someone. My father's letter, apparently, had been the first to arrive for an eternity. — My father, of course, wanted to introduce her, as he'd done for all the invited readers to date. (He always stood at the front, at the lectern, his eyes screwed shut as if the light were blinding him — it was blinding him — his legs twisted like two stems of wisteria. He'd speak quietly, looking for the right words, as if he weren't in the least prepared. In fact, he'd have prepared his little speech rather *too* well.) — Today, this evening, he felt so unwell, however, that — with, literally, the last of his strength — he phoned the school Principal and asked him to step in for him. To apologize to the poet for him. (Whom he admired.) After that call, he heard the child, his now long-since adult son, me, coming down the stairs, opened the door and said he wasn't well, wasn't at all well. 'Could you stay at home this evening?' — 'But Papa,' I said. 'You know we've tickets for the circus.' He nodded, and my mother and I set off. (Clara loved circuses. Attending the poetry reading, and not Circus Knie's Gala Evening, didn't even occur to us as a possibility. Not to me, at least.) — My father was sitting in the easy chair, listening — for the third time that day — to the Bach cantata 'Ich habe genug'. He was crying, now he was alone. The room was growing darker and darker, he hadn't turned the lamp on, and didn't have the strength to get up and flick the switch. Everything was hurting, every muscle in his body, every nerve, his heart. He remembered times past, walking in hail and lightning to his father's village. The singing competition in the Black Chapel. The lantern procession across to the inn. The jostling at the coffins, outside the door. The dancing. The night in the barn. He made a sound, a bit like a laugh. He looked at the clock — the gramophone silent now — and felt a sudden yearning to go into town after all, and welcome the poet. He stood up and took a few steps. He was dizzy, but when he took deep breaths the stars before his eyes went away again. He leant against the door frame, to steady himself. His head was hammering, his heart struggling. He left the house, stumbled to the tram stop, using fences and the walls of houses for support, travelled into the centre and was soon standing in Restaurant Paradies, where, since the very first reading — Heinrich Böll had read to an audience of twenty-one — he'd always gone after the event with the poet, or poetess, and the hard core of enthusiasts. He reckoned the Principal would do the same and, indeed, did find the usual group at the big table, over which a miniature Carnival lantern the Surrealist had once

painted hung. (He hadn't been in the Ticino, either, since the
scandal involving Kirchner's pupil, preferring, instead, to go
to Paradies when in town.) At the head of the table, facing my
father, sat a woman, a cross between a lady and a witch,
the poet, of course. She jumped up, as if recognizing the new
arrival, and everyone turned around. Stared at him as if he
was a ghost. He, probably, was one; looked like one — he was
wearing his cardigan though it was a hot summer's night —
and the Principal got up and rushed over to him. 'Are you all
right?' he asked, taking him by the elbow. He introduced him
to the poet, and my father stammered that he hadn't been well,
up until just now, but then hadn't been able to resist the temptation of meeting her. And here he was. — She smiled. The
reading had been lovely, something of a pathetic triumph, the
assembly hall so full that people who had travelled specially
from Berne or Brig — the poet never read; not ever! — had to
be turned away. On the floor, on the stage, on the windowsills:
readers had been sitting everywhere, keen to hear her. — Now,
the poet wasn't tired at all but full of beans. My father, who
had sat down beside her, also picked up. He ordered a glass
of wine, and drank a few sips. At midnight, they had to leave,
it was closing time, and my father, almost healthy now,
insisted on accompanying the poet to her hotel. (For the first
time, he'd used the Hotel zum Schwert, where Mozart,
Napoleon and Bartók had all stayed, as the price reflected.)
They walked along the river, discussing poems, that is, how
they rarely worked out for them, and, if they did, you didn't
know why or how. They stood at the hotel entrance. The river,
black, flowed past. They were silent. Finally, the poet said,
'We have met once before.' My father looked at her, wonder-
ing. 'On your twelfth birthday. At the celebration. I should
have liked to dance with you. But didn't.'

'You are the blacksmith's daughter,' my father said. 'If only I had known!'

'You do now.'

With astonishing agility she gave him something like a kiss and went into the hotel. My father stared at the door as it closed, slowly, turned and walked, along the river, to the tram stop. The last tram was long since gone, of course, so he took a taxi. As he entered the house, every nerve in his head began to rage, and he realized he'd not felt any pain earlier. Clara and the child were in bed, sleeping; there wasn't a sound from their rooms, at least. He was quiet, too. He opened the white book, wrote the first half of a sentence, but was then too exhausted and postponed that day's entry until the next morning. He swallowed his many pills, and an extra Librium, and yet woke, if, indeed, he had been asleep, in the middle of the night again. It was still dark outside, though it was June. 18 June 1965. He lit a cigarette and went to the bathroom, turned on a tap, and collapsed, dead, or nearly dead, only a little alive still, when his son, me, a few seconds later, appeared before him.

LESS THAN TWO HOURS LATER, I drove off in my Citroën 2CV. I was looking for my father's village, to fetch his coffin. I'd never been there, but found it right away on my road map. No problem, it wasn't as if it was far away. It was a beautiful summer's morning, I'd the car roof down and drove, my elbow out the window, towards the mid-mountains. First, along the lake; then inland, which was getting more and more mountainous. Hardly any traffic; here and there, I overtook a tractor or a few cyclists. For a while, I drove along an avenue, straight as a poker, lined by poplars. The engine made that rasping sound that only Citroëns did, or do. As if someone were kicking cans down the street. I don't know why but I was close to singing. Because the vault of the sky was so blue, so luminous? —I entered a valley, on a road that, like the valley itself, was getting narrower and narrower. On a bend, I found myself nose to nose with a post bus, the driver of which, thank God, had used his horn. A brand-new Saurer bus, with a panorama windscreen, whose driver gave me a friendly wave when I reversed and pulled in.—Then the road climbed steeply, winding its way up the mountain. Streams passed beneath me, foaming. Pines, Swiss stone pines, mossy rocks. On the tight bends, I'd to go back down into first gear each time, and even on the straight stretches of road didn't get above second.—Once, a marmot whistled, then a deer leapt into the forest.—The road then became flat, followed a roaring mountain stream and eventually passed a rock formation, four limestone towers, rising into the sky. A gentle curve, and already I was among barns and houses made of dark wood, at the top end of the village square, an arena that went down such a steep slope, I'd to go down into first again. I drove down to the inn, where two or three other cars were already parked outside. When I got out of the car, I could see, a bit above me, the Black Chapel, which wasn't black at all but white-washed. The weathercock, golden, was shining in the sun.—The inn was beaming, a similarly pure white (perhaps the landlord and the pastor had joined forces, to buy the paint for the renovations), and green flowerboxes, full of geraniums, had been put in all the windows. A neon sign (yellow, 'Cardinal Beer') above the glass door that opened, automatically, when I approached it. A big room with lots of tables. White tablecloths, napkins folded to look like a cardinal's hat. Not a soul, not behind the counter either, over which—

as yellow as outside—another Cardinal sign was suspended.
I opened a door in the wall opposite to see a hall that was so
dark that I could only make out the vague outlines of tables and
chairs. Some kind of storeroom, more like: gigantic, smelling of
dust.—I went back to the counter; called 'Anyone there?'—
Almost immediately, a man was in front of me, young, strong,
with a pile of plates in his hands, that he put down on the
counter. 'Yes?' he said.—'Is the landlord here?' I said.—'I am
the landlord.'—'I'm Karl's son,' I said. 'I've come to fetch his
coffin.'—'Whose son?' The landlord looked at me. 'What was
that about a coffin?'—'My father's coffin. It's here, with all
the rest.'—The landlord scratched his head and began to
laugh. 'I remember now,' he said. 'The coffins outside the
house. As children, we played at being dead in them.' He drew
a beer. 'When we did the conversion—my father was still in
charge then—we made firewood of all that junk.' He pushed
the beer towards me, and I drank a large gulp.—'But the
coffins! There are a few outside every house here.'—'Not any
more. Not for a long time now,' the landlord said. 'A few thousand tourists come here every year. Imagine: you're Japanese,
you've paid all that money to make the trip, you want things to
be nice, and then you're tripping over coffins wherever you
go.'—'See what you mean,' I said, and emptied my glass.—
'Outside the forge, there's still a box like that. It's private prop-
erty. So the community can't do anything about it. All the rest
have gone.'—I nodded, didn't say anything, looked around the
room. On the walls were pictures with farming scenes, no
kitsch, and if there was it was contemporary.—'We're related
to one another,' I said. 'Your grandfather was my father's
father's brother.'—'Right,' the landlord said, shaking my hand
across the counter. He laughed. I turned and went to the
door. As it slid open, he called over, 'Two-eighty.'—'Pardon?' I

stopped. — 'The beer,' he said. I paid and gave him a generous tip. Then I started the Citroën's engine and drove, in first, up the rock wall of the square, at full throttle, and still not doing even twenty. It was only on the village street the engine got going, and I moved up into third as I passed the forge that I recognized by its coffin; the only coffin, far and wide. The wood grey with age; black, nearly. — Two or three hours later, I was home again, though I stopped at the restaurant at the Old Customs, ate some bread and sausage, and drank another beer, in its beer garden beneath the chestnuts. A few workers from the factory, whose shift was over; and, in one corner, a couple in love, holding hands and smiling at one another, diagonally, across the table. — Back home, without the coffin, I found a note on the floor from Clara, from my mother. She didn't want to sleep with a dead man, and was at Hildegard's. — My dead father was no longer in the house, though; I'd arranged myself — with it being well over thirty degrees, meanwhile, in the shade — for him to be taken away immediately. And yet I shivered when I looked around his room. The couch, carefully covered with its Arabic- or Russian-looking throw, as if nothing had changed. The bedside table. The book on it, that my father had just been reading (H. C. Artmann's *Verbarium*). The desk. The Bigla one, on it his Sachs-Vilatte and other dictionaries. The bookshelves round the walls, and the cabinet for his author's copies. The window. The door to the terrace. The door to the bathroom, still open. — On the desk lay his white book and, of course, I leafed through it. I was allowed to now; had to, even. I stared at his beautiful, precise handwriting and, here and there, read a word or half a sentence. The letters were so small that my nose was touching the paper as I read. Finally, I read the last entry but didn't know what to make of it: '*17 June 1965. Lovely evening*

after all. I now know her name.' —Who did he mean? —Then I
leafed through the papers on the desk a little—the unan-
swered letters were piling up, notes, publishers' catalogues—
and, at random, took a book from his archive. Just like that.
Coincidentally, it was the *L'Éducation sentimentale*, and so,
standing at the shelf still, I read the final page, words, the
sense of which Flaubert had determined but that my father
had written. The passage, in which Frédéric, after all those
years, comes back to the dump he grew up in, and recalls
how, as an adolescent, an eternity ago, he'd dared to enter the
anteroom of the local brothel and then—barely had he set eyes
on one of the ladies, even from a distance—run straight back
out again. 'That was the best time we ever had', he says to his
friend Deslauriers, who agrees with him, yes, all their lives,
but that, indeed, was the best time. —I put the book back. I'd
now tears in my eyes, after all. I emptied the contents of the
medication drawer onto the couch. A hundred or more little
jars, tubes or boxes full of medicines. Treupel to keep him
going for a few years; so much Librium that you'd think he
shovelled it down him, but plasters and ointments and little
bottles, too, the content of which had evaporated and whose
labels I couldn't read. No revolver. Had he thrown it away?
Into the lake, by night? Into a thicket in the forest? And
when? —The drawers in the desk contained the expected bits
and pieces. Paper clips, postage stamps, rubber bands, rubbers, pencils. The very top drawer was still locked. No key,
nowhere. I fetched a hammer and a chisel and burst the lock
open. The drawer was filled with envelopes, so many, in fact,
a number, freed from the pressure, jumped out of the drawer
and fell to the ground. Without exception, the letters were still
sealed, as the postman had delivered them—postmarks that
went back ten and more years—and they all contained bills,

as I saw when I began to open them. Unpaid bills. All of them! My father had never misjudged things and allowed a real letter to vanish, unopened. (Clara later paid the bills. Many, of them, in any case. A total of about thirty thousand francs.) — No secret novel. No love letters. No porno mags. Only at the very bottom, concealed beneath the already historic bills, lay, behind glass and framed, the black and white photo of a female torso, of a naked woman, at the top of which you could just about see the beginning of her neck and, at the bottom, her pubic hair and a tiny bit of her thighs. The cloth, white silk, perhaps, that she was lying on. An amateur photo, very clearly, not a bought one. Who was the woman? Hélène, about whom my father had told me? One of his unknown flames from many years back? Or my mother, young? — I'd no desire either to sleep, all on my own, in the dead man's house, and so drove into town, to Isabelle, who came — and still does come — from Les-Entre-Deux-Monts, in the Jura region, and whom I'd known for barely a fortnight. She was pleased when I rang her doorbell, and alarmed when I told her my father had died. (She'd seen him only once, hardly a week ago, and he'd immediately begun babbling in a French more fluent than I'd expected of him: for decades already, a silent philologist. Probably, she reminded him of Hélène. She seemed to like him too, and so they spoke for a long time, leaving me out of it, about French cheeses, both were astonishingly knowledgeable.) — The next day I returned to the house, later than planned. I parked the Citroën in the shade of a gigantic fir in the neighbour's garden. My mother was out on the pavement, at the garden gate, watching the bin lorry that, right at that moment, far below, was vanishing round the corner. She was wearing her blue apron and, while pale in the face, as white as chalk, was full of energy. She went back into the house, ahead of me, at the speed of a Herr Wagner or Kern, at any rate. I followed her, up the stairs, into my father's study. A half-full 50-litre rubbish bag was in the middle of the room, and my mother took a—*another*—pack of paper from the Bigla and stuffed it into the bag. 'I started without you,' she said, 'to tidy up. You can't imagine what a mess it was.'— I went over to the desk. The many letters or publishers' catalogues were gone, and for the first time I could see the surface of the desk that—how could I have expected black, high-grade timber?—was made of ugly linoleum. Brownish-grey patterning, covered with ink stains—and burns, caused by cigarette ash. The bills were there, in three carefully ordered piles, without their envelopes now: pay, perhaps pay, don't pay. The typewriter, a green Olivetti, the third or fourth in a string of Olivetti's he'd bought, attracted by their *italianità*, perhaps, though he destroyed them faster than any other machines. The keys tended not to survive his index finger; not for very long. Those on a Remington, a Continental or an Adler didn't, either. (In thirty years, he'd no doubt wrecked just as many typewriters and, on a few occasions, also his index finger. He then had to use his middle finger for a few months.) Beside, behind, the typewriter, or on either side of it: two framed photos; one, of a young Clara, serious and very beautiful, standing outside the Historical Museum; the other, of two boys in sailor suits, his brother, Felix, and him. (Felix had died before him, abandoned by his heart.) The two wooden sculptures from Africa, the man with the red stump of a penis and the woman with the white V between her legs. A paperweight: a Dürer-style hare, made of black bronze. Two pencils. An inkpot with the quill in it.—Where was the white book? My heart began to race. 'Where's the white book?' I said.—'I told you, sure,' Clara said, bent over the bottom drawer of the Bigla. 'In the rubbish. The first lot's already been taken away, thank God.'—'You threw away the white book?' I said, I screamed. 'Why?'—My mother didn't answer me, pulled an ancient-looking leather bag with two handles, a thing that looked like an archaic rucksack, out from in a corner, and stuffed it, too, into the rubbish bag. 'Phew!' she said, wiping the sweat from her brow.—I stormed out the door and, boiling with anger, walked up and down the garden. That said, when, half an hour, or a whole hour later, my mother dragged the rubbish bags one after another to the door to the garden, I did go up and help her. Paper is heavy. There they stood, the rubbish bags, along the garden wall, next to one another, black, their heads lolling forward, as if executed —The funeral was two days later. A lot of people, the funeral service hall was crammed full. The first violist of the Young Orchestra (the only person in the Young Orchestra, with whom Clara was still in contact, and who had agreed, immediately, to come) played with considerable brio a piece by Bach arranged for solo viola. A young clergyman spoke, in black, yes, and with a white collar; but not at all clergy-like. He'd been a pupil of my father's, and it was clear to him he was burying someone who didn't believe in Paradise. Many other former pupils attended, serious, young, and—of course—a few of his colleagues. The school Principal, who also held a short speech. Clara sat in the front row, her lips trembling. Me beside her, Isabelle. I could see Jo, further away, and beside her. Nina, accompanied by the man she'd been living with for twenty years already. (Hildegard couldn't come—she sent a huge bouquet of flowers—because her employer, Edwin Schimmel, on this, of all afternoons, had urgent letters to dictate.)—The Surrealist and the lady painter were sitting next to one another; Herr Fenster was there, too.

Albert Züst, Heinrich Böll, Klaus Nonnenmann. Fräulein Doktor had come, alone, though she never went anywhere without Nobs. The lyric poet had also come, was sitting right at the back, with a silk scarf round her head. (No one from my father's village had come.) — The editors of both the local newspapers, and a few from the radio. Even Myrta and Arnulf were sitting, in black, in one of the front rows, though neither my father nor Clara had seen them in recent years. And while the organ was playing a closing chorale, and everyone was reaching for their hats and gloves, a small dog trotted in the door and up to the coffin, a little bundle of grey hair, and for a moment I thought, Hobby, my God, Hobby's come back. — Afterwards, everyone went to the restaurant opposite the cemetery. Cold cuts and wine were served. I sat between my mother and Isabelle; and soon the mourners — laughing more and more often, and more and more cheerfully — were exchanging memories of the dead man. The way he could rage! How he'd been able to galvanize them! — Isabelle had to return, that same evening, to the part of the country where she grew up — she, too, had parents; in Les-Entre-Deux-Monts — so I walked her to the bus. We waited, and when the bus appeared in the distance, I told her that I — yes, that I was going to re-write my father's book; his white book; that *I* would now write it, in order to read it; to be the first to. Then she would get to see it, and after her, as is the custom, everyone else. — I kissed Isabelle, she boarded the bus, and the bus drove off.